Award Winning Tips to Build Energy Efficient Homes

Profit *from* Building Green

Jeannie Leggett Sikora

National Association of Home Builders Research Center

Profit from Building Green:
Award Winning Tips to Build Energy Efficient Homes
National Association of Home Builders Research Center
Jeannie Leggett Sikora

ISBN 0-86718-524-4
© 2002 by BuilderBooks™
of the National Association of Home Builders of the United States of America

Cover Design by Tim Kaage, LaurelGraphx
Printed in the United States of America

Cataloging-in-Publication Data available from the Library of Congress

Disclaimer
This publication is designed to provide accurate and authoritative information in regard to the subject matter covered. It is sold with the understanding that the publisher is not engaged in rendering legal, accounting, or other professional service. If legal advice or other expert assistance is required, the services of a competent professional person should be sought.
—From a Declaration of Principles jointly adopted by a Committee of the American Bar Association and a Committee of Publishers and Associations.

This report was prepared as an account of work sponsored by an agency of the United States government. Neither the United States government nor any agency thereof, nor any of their employees, makes any warranty, express or implied, or assumes any legal liability or responsibility for the accuracy, completeness, or usefulness of any information, apparatus, product, or process disclosed, or represents that its use would not infringe privately owned rights. Reference herein to any specific commercial product, process, or service by trade name, trademark, manufacturer, or otherwise does not necessarily constitute or imply its endorsement, recommendation, or favoring by the United States government or any agency thereof. The views and opinions of authors expressed herein do not necessarily state or reflect those of the United States government or any agency thereof. Publication #: NREL/SR-550-28996; subcontract number AAX-1-30482-01. Also available electronically at http://www.doe.gov/bridge.

Publication #: NREL/SR-550-28996; subcontract number AAX-1-30482-01.

For more information:
BuilderBooks™
National Association of Home Builders
1201 15th Street, NW
Washington, DC 20005-2800
(800) 223-2665
Check us out online at **www.builderbooks.com**

11/01 T. Minch/Bang Printing 1500

Contents

List of Figures

1 Energy- and Resource-Efficient Design

2 Energy-Efficient Building Systems

3 Energy- and Resource-Efficient C onstruction

4 Cutting-Edge Technologies

5 Marketing Energy- and Resource-Efficient Homes

About the NAHB Research Center, Inc.

The NAHB Research Center is the research and development leader in the home building industry, dedicated to advancing housing technology and enhancing housing affordability for the benefit of all Americans. Federal, state, and local government agencies, manufacturers, builders, and remodelers rely on the expertise and objectivity that are at the very heart of the Research Center.

The key objectives of the NAHB Research Center are:
· Conducting research on the frontiers of building technology for the benefit of the home building industry and people who live in American-built homes.
· Promoting high standards of quality in building materials and construction.
· Keeping the American home building industry in a top competitive position in this country and throughout the world.

Reasons for our success include:
· Our programs are results oriented.
· Our ties to NAHB provide constant contact with the real world of home building.
· Our research and development flow directly into the building industry.

The NAHB Research Center is on the cutting edge of housing research, always striving to solve today's problems and advance tomorrow's housing.

About the Author

Jeannie Leggett Sikora has worked at the NAHB Research Center as a research engineer since 1997. Her primary focus is improving energy efficiency and promoting the use of renewable energy in new homes.

Prior to working at the NAHB Research Center, Ms. Sikora served as an educator in the dairy industry at the University of Wisconsin and Penn State; first developing outreach materials about on-farm biogas production at Penn State and subsequently working in Wisconsin with dairy farmers and dairy processors to increase energy efficiency in the industry. She holds a Bachelor's of Science degree from Lehigh University and a Master of Science degree from Penn State. Ms. Sikora resides in Annapolis, Maryland with her husband and son.

Acknowledgments

Contributors

Significant contributions were made to this document by Cameron Duncan, Karen M. Johnson, Kevin Powell, Karin Victorio, and Donna Woodhurst. The guide was reviewed and edited by Christopher J. Fennell, Carol Soble, and National Renewable Energy Laboratory staff Ren Anderson, Kyra Epstein, Sheila Hayter, Ron Judkoff, and Paul Torcellini. Funding for this work was provided by the U.S. Department of Energy Office of Building Technology, State, and Community Programs' Building America Program through the National Renewable Energy Laboratory.

Book Preparation

This book is produced under the general direction of Jerry Howard, NAHB Executive Vice President and CEO, in association with NAHB staff members Michael Shibley, Executive Vice President, Builder, Associate & Affiliate Services; Greg French, Staff Vice President, Publications and Non-dues Revenues; Eric Johnson, Publisher, BuilderBooks; Theresa Minch, Acquisitions Editor; David Rhodes, Art and Production Director; and Toral Patel, Assistant Editor.

Introduction

Residential and commercial buildings account for about one-third of all the energy used in the United States. As concern over the environment grows, builders have the potential to fulfill a market niche by building homes that use fewer resources and have lower environmental impact than conventional construction.

Builders can increase their marketability and customer satisfaction and, at the same time, reduce the environmental impact of their homes. However, it takes dedication to build environmentally sound homes along with a solid marketing approach to ensure that customers recognize the added value of energy and resource efficiency.

In many cases, builders and industry professionals have to learn new techniques, identify new products, and educate customers about the benefits of energy and resource efficiency. Although consumer awareness and concern over the environment is growing, knowledge of energy-efficient construction and its environmental benefits is not widespread. Therefore, it is often the energy-efficient builder's responsibility to educate consumers to increase market demand.

This book is intended for builders seeking suggestions on how to improve energy and resource efficiency in their new homes. It is a compilation of ideas and concepts for designing, building, and marketing energy- and resource-efficient homes based on the experiences from the recipients of the national EnergyValue Housing Award (EVHA). The award recognizes builders for their voluntary efforts to incorporate

> *Any house plan can be made more energy efficient. You don't need a designer, you just need to know a little about how a house works as a system.*
>
> — **Bruno Zagar,** State of the Art Builders

1

energy and resource efficiency into the design, construction, technology, and marketing of their new homes.

Exemplary builders of energy- and resource-efficient homes offer their customers a comfortable and affordable place to live. In return, builders earn the good will of their customers, enjoy the satisfaction of producing a high-quality, environmentally friendly product, and take advantage of the opportunity to carve out a niche market. Given that home buyers have increasingly easy access to information about construction practices, the marketing of energy efficiency is an ideal way to make buyers take notice.

A comprehensive approach to energy- and resource-efficient home construction is suited to all types—from affordable to luxury homes in hot, humid, or extremely cold climates, and everything in between. This comprehensive approach involves considering conditions related to solar heat gain and prevailing winds, eliminating drafts and cold spots through air sealing, carefully placing insulation to avoid gaps, and providing fresh air inside the home.

Becoming a successful builder of energy-efficient homes is more than just learning new building techniques; it is also about implementing innovative designs and technologies, high-quality construction practices, and creative marketing campaigns.

I n the seven years since the EnergyValue Housing Awards (EVHA) program started, EVHA-winning applicants have increasingly featured resource-efficient and environmentally sensitive land development in their homes. From developing urban infill sites and picking sites close to public transportation, to including recycling centers in kitchens and planting native, drought-resistant landscaping, the builders who have excelled in this awards program demonstrate sensitivity to the environmental impact of homes throughout the life cycle.

As a result of this applicant-driven growth in the resource-efficiency focus of EVHA, a new awards program has been created to succeed the EVHA. This new awards program, *The National Green Building Awards*, addresses the escalating interest in green building by recognizing exemplary builders, manufacturers, institutions, and others. For more information about *The National Green Building Awards*, visit the NAHB Research Center's Web site at www.nahbrc.org or contact the program coordinator at ngba@nahbrc.org.

The practices adopted by the EVHA-winning builders offer simple and effective strategies for designing, constructing, and marketing energy- and resource-efficient homes. This guide outlines many of the practices, offers practical tips on how to get involved in energy-efficient construction, and provides innovative sales ideas for marketing unique homes in a competitive marketplace.

Energy- and Resource-Efficient Design

Some people have a typecast image of an energy-efficient home as one with huge, unattractive solar panels and strange gadgets. In fact, energy-efficient homes do not have to relegate aesthetics to second place—in many cases, energy-efficient homes look identical to conventional homes.

Incorporating an energy-efficient design may require added thought, time, and money, but it may not be as difficult as you think. A home's efficiency may be enhanced by simply improving air-sealing practices, taking steps to reduce air infiltration and increase insulation levels, or switching to energy-efficient windows and doors. For more complicated changes, you may want to consult a builder, architect, or engineer who specializes in energy efficiency. Turn to the design section to read about design considerations in more detail.

Energy-Efficient Building Systems

The variety of building products and the new products manufactures introduce every year can be overwhelming. The building systems section presents a selection of energy efficient technologies that have been successful for EVHA winners.

Although the products described are not inclusive of all the available options, the major areas of construction are covered. The resource lists of organizations, manufacturers, and terminology found at the end of the book will help readers who would like more information about energy efficiency building materials and technologies.

Energy- and Resource-Efficient Construction

Once you have decided on energy-efficient features and design, it is important that all participants in the construction process understand these features and the purpose behind them. Conscientious construction crews are vital to the design's effectiveness—taking short cuts can undermine energy-efficient design. Detailed plans help contractors understand how to implement efficiency measures. A knowledgeable manager who oversees construction can also help reduce the number of errors and the quantity of wasted material. Although successful energy-efficient construction practices require careful implementation, they are not necessarily more complicated than conventional practices.

Consult the construction section to learn more about how EVHA-winning builders are using energy-efficient technologies and innovative designs in the field.

Marketing Energy- and Resource-Efficient Homes

Customer buy-in through education is crucial to the successful sale of energy-efficient homes. Because energy-efficient designs do not necessarily look different from less efficient homes, innovative marketing techniques help ensure that prospective buyers recognize all of the advantages of buying an energy-efficient home.

Some EVHA winning builders use model cutaways of wall sections, take prospective buyers on CD-ROM virtual home tours, guarantee energy costs, and use customer testimonials in newspaper advertisements. Most builders team up with local utilities or the federal ENERGY STAR™ program to help promote energy efficiency. E Seal utility members offer innovative financing to make it easier for homeowners to buy energy-efficient homes. These and similar programs help demonstrate to the homeowner that enhanced energy efficiency reduces monthly utility costs. See the marketing section for more ideas on creative marketing techniques.

Using the Guide

By illustrating examples set by EVHA-winning builders, this guide can help you decide which practices you would like to adopt and how to start implementing them. It outlines successful strategies used by builders and identifies barriers to adopting EVHA-winning practices. Most important, you can discover how builders use their energy- and resource-efficient designs to win loyal customers and gain a competitive edge.

Chapter One

Energy- and Resource-Efficient Design

Designing an energy- and resource-efficient home requires more planning than a conventionally designed home. When choosing features for an efficient home, designers need to consider local climate, the building site, available resources, the cost versus added value of efficiency upgrades, and aesthetics.

Climate-specific energy-efficient considerations include local temperatures and the amount and angle of solar radiation. For example, in southern regions of the United States, energy-efficient architecture minimizes solar heat gain during a large portion of the year while in northern climates, energy-efficient designs make use of solar heat gain. Climate often dictates what energy-efficient features are practical and cost effective. A design that works in a hot, humid region might fail or prove impractical in a cold climate.

In addition, a resource-efficient home depends on the local availability of resources. For example, water is a more precious resource in Phoenix than in Seattle. In cloudy regions, the specification of low-energy appliances and compact fluorescent lamps might represent a more efficient use of resources than photovoltaic solar panels. The use of locally available building materials can mean a more productive use of resources than importing materials from distant places.

Simple design decisions can have a major impact on the energy and resource efficiency of a new home and its ultimate affordability. For example, placing ductwork within the conditioned space of a home and centrally locating the HVAC equipment reduces the amount of required ductwork and limits the energy loss from leaky ducts. A house tightly sealed against air infiltration and insulated to a high R-value can reduce the total amount of energy needed for heating and cooling as well as reduce HVAC equipment size and initial system cost.

While many energy-efficient features add to the cost of a home, some save money and resources. The use of power-vented, sealed-combustion furnaces eliminates the need for a chimney. The cost of building a chimney far outweighs the additional cost of the furnace.

Ultimately, the builder decides what features are cost effective, marketable, and logical for a given region and market. The techniques described in this guide can be implemented in part or in total. However, it is important to remember that a house is a system and that changes made to one part of the system could affect other parts of the system. It is the builder's responsibility to make sure a home's system is the best one for the targeted customer.

Minimizing Building Loads

The first step to improving energy efficiency is reducing the amount of energy needed to keep a home comfortable. Heating and cooling loads are a function of building size, solar gains, air infiltration, interior loads from people and appliances, humidity, and the difference between indoor and outdoor temperatures. Several ways to minimize heating and cooling loads include minimizing the house size, shading with landscaping or overhangs, protecting against air infiltration with windbreaks and air-sealing practices, and installing energy-efficient appliances.

Indoor Air Quality

A common practice among builders of energy-efficient homes is to make residences as airtight as possible by using air barriers, caulking, foam, gaskets, and other methods to minimize drafts and outdoor air infiltration. However, if a home is too tight, pollutants cannot escape and indoor air quality (IAQ) can be compromised. To ensure high IAQ, Christian Builders of Rogers, Minn., introduced several features to its tight homes.

Figure 1.1 *A heat recovery ventilator brings fresh air into a house without sacrificing energy efficiency.*

Figure 1.2 *Spray foam insulation can be used between a garage and the home to make an air barrier that isolates the home from the carbon monoxide produced in a garage.*

To begin, Christian uses paint without VOCs and specifies low-VOC varnishes. These products do not generate as much odor as conventional paints and finishes. The company's use of solid wood cabinetry eliminates the potential threat of formaldehyde off-gassing associated with particleboard cabinets. They vent their homes' garages to release any carbon monoxide directly to the outdoors. Finally, but most importantly, Christian installs a heat recovery ventilator (HRV) that brings a constant supply of fresh air into the home as it recovers energy from the outgoing air.

It should be noted that homes with ventilation systems can have higher fuel bills than those without such systems because a ventilation system depends on outdoor air to replace conditioned air. HRVs can recover about 70 percent of the energy leaving a building. And, according to Brad Richardson of Christian Builders, the results are worth it. Richardson says, "Although the fuel bills are little higher [than an energy-efficient home without ventilation], nobody has ever complained. Customers like that the fresh air is free of odors and condensation. Most customers want to find out what the equipment is doing, how it works, and how to maintain it."

Richardson notes that the increased costs of ensuring a fresh supply of indoor air presents a problem in entry-level homes where the added cost is even higher as a percent of the total home cost. He estimates that for a $125,000 home, the IAQ package costs $3,000 to $5,000. Unfortunately, there is no concrete financial payback.

Christian Builders started paying special attention to IAQ in 1994 when a woman with chemical sensitivities asked the company to build her a house. To build that first house, Christian Builders contacted a local supplier of efficiency equipment, the local HBA, and the University of Minnesota. Initially, the builder had to sell its subcontractors on the new approach, but now Richardson says the subcontractors sometimes recommend approaches to him.

To ensure that techniques are implemented properly, the firm's superintendent makes frequent visits to each house and performs a final inspection. The extra fieldwork helps identify problems that would be more difficult to fix later. All the efficiency measures that Christian Builders incorporate into its homes take a little extra planning, implementation time, and expense. Nonetheless, Richardson says, "Service problems are virtually eliminated and durability is improved. For example, in a very cold climate, our windows don't have mold or condensation problems. We provide comfort and our clients recognize that."

Maximizing Solar Energy Use

We all know what it's like to get into a car that has been sitting in the sun. Even when the outdoor temperature is low, it's warm inside. That's passive solar energy at work. By designing and building with the sun in mind, we can create homes that are heated and lighted primarily by solar energy and cooled naturally by shading and

Figures 1.3 and **1.4** *Passive solar homes can be both attractive and traditional in appearance. These two attractive solar homes take full advantage of solar heat gain and shading to minimize unwanted heat gain during the summer months.*

8

ventilation. Passive solar design can dramatically reduce energy use and costs for heating and cooling without adversely affecting the comfort level in your home.

Passive solar design uses natural architectural features to maximize winter solar heat gain, minimize summer heat gain, and provide light and ventilation. South-facing windows are sized for solar gain, north-facing windows provide ventilation and natural light, and east- and west-facing windows are avoided. Overhangs will shade the windows from the summer sun and the window placement permits natural ventilation.

Figure 1.5 *Sign at the front of an all passive solar subdivision.*

Good solar design usually starts with orienting the long side of a house along an east-west axis; however, optimal site layout is not always possible when working within the confines of a site plan. As any builder knows, optimal siting competes with other variables such as topography and the location of utilities. It is best to get an early start on solar design because ideal solar orientation can be nearly impossible when a plot is already developed.

One company from Oneida, Wisc., State of the Art Builders, incorporated passive solar heating and daylighting into all 35 homes in a subdivision. Siting and zoning were not an issue because the land developer wanted to make the use of solar energy a priority. However, according to State of the Art's Bruno Zagar, builders need to work with developers because covenants often restrict siting, orientation, or components of solar energy systems, including photovoltaic or solar hot water panels. Zagar advises builders to be proactive with their municipal and county planning and zoning offices. He recommends going to local HBA meetings to talk about restrictive covenants and bring photographs of EVHA-winning homes to demonstrate that solar design is not unattractive and frequently looks no different than conventional design.

Passive solar design, while simple in concept, requires cal-

culations to deter-
mine window and
overhang sizes. Cit-
ing issues such as
glare, correct lighting
levels, and climate-
specific window se-
lection, Zagar notes
that the design of a
passive solar home
requires that either a
builder or architect
experienced with so-
lar energy issues
is involved.

> *To make designing passive solar homes easier in your community, be proactive with municipal and county planning/zoning offices. Go to local HBA meetings, talk about restrictive covenants, and bring photographs of EVHA-winning homes to demonstrate that solar design is not unattractive and frequently looks no different than conventional designs.*
>
> *– Bruno Zagar, State of the Art Builders*

To incorporate an extensive energy-efficiency package in its EVHA-winning home, State of the Art Builders spent approximately $5,400 more than in the case of a conventional home. The package, which included low-E, argon-filled wood windows, slab insulation, air sealing, extra insulation, HRV, raised-heel roof trusses, passive solar heating, and daylighting, rewarded the Wisconsin homeowner with a $200 annual heating bill.

Energy-Efficient Landscaping

On a hot, sunny summer day, a wooded area can provide respite from the heat. Just as people are cooler in the shade, so too are houses. Landscaping design can help improve energy efficiency by protecting homes from the summer sun as much as from blustery winter winds. A little extra planning can mean a landscape plan that reduces energy bills and increases comfort. A more elaborate type of landscape design called xeriscaping conserves water and minimizes the need for chemical input.

Simple landscaping for energy efficiency calls for leaving tall trees standing, shading outdoor air-conditioning units, minimizing shading on the southern exposure, and planting deciduous trees near south- or southwest-facing windows and evergreen trees near north- or northwest-facing windows (to block drafts). All of these strategies are simple and low- or no-cost methods for reducing heating and cooling costs. Xeriscaping involves a little more background research and planning to determine the best plants for a given region.

Emerald Homes of Houston has always enjoyed a niche as an energy-efficient builder. In a patio-home development, the firm wanted to introduce several strategies for lowering the cost of operating a home. To reduce yard work and outdoor maintenance costs, Emerald Homes chose hardy, drought-tolerant native plants such as Burford holly and Texas sage that don't require much chemical input. In addition, the firm planted shrubbery appropriate for the climate and selected a special buffalo grass that doesn't need much water.

Brian Binash of Emerald Homes says that drought-tolerant

landscaping did not cost that much more than traditional landscaping. "The cost is in the homework," Binash says. "You have to want to go out of your way to learn. It's the same as with other energy efficiency measures."

Woody Cady Photo

Figure 1.6 *The builder of this low-input landscape left many large trees standing. The trees help shade the area, keeping houses cooler and landscaping moist.*

To learn about plants adapted to a dry climate, Emerald worked with landscape architects and landscapers and performed some of its own research. Some plants did cost more, says Binash. Container-grown trees, which have a higher post-planting survival rate, each cost about $100 more than comparably sized trees.

Because the homes in the patio-home development were zero-lot-line units, Emerald found it relatively easy to implement drought-tolerant landscaping. Though Binash warns, "Land plans don't always lend themselves to minimal-input landscaping. We were able to do it because the lots were small and had minimal exposure to the sun."

Although it might be difficult to implement full-scale xeriscaping, no- or low-cost energy-efficient landscaping plans .

11

can be used in any climate. To find out about plants native to your region, check with your local university cooperative extension office, a landscape architect, or your landscaper. In-depth information can be found in the landscaping books cited in the Green Building Resources appendix.

Chapter Two

Energy-Efficient Building Systems

The variety of building products and methods available to builders is astounding. Each prodcut or process sepcified by a builder reflects a calculated decision that balances cost, perfomrance, and aesthetics. Energy- and resource-efficient construction technologies are no different. This guide helps simplify some of those decisions by outlining technologies and practices used successfully by nationally renowned builders of energy- and resource efficient homes.

E nergy- and resource-efficient construction technologies sometimes apply concepts that are new to local building officials. To avoid problems, meet with your local code official before the permit stage. If needed, provide input from a local architect or engineer, or present your own data. The resources in the back of this book also can provide more information.

Although not inclusive of all the available options, the guide covers the major areas of construction and provides a list of resources that directs readers to more information. The ideas presented here can be incorporated into affordable or luxury homes and, in most cases, are suited to any climatic region.

Alternative Wall Systems

Advanced Framing Techniques

By using advanced framing or optimum value eengineering (OVE) techniques, a builder can save up to $1,000 in material costs on a 2,400-square-foot house and 3 percent to 5 percent on framing labor costs while saving the homeowner about 2 percent to 3 percent in annual heating and cooling costs. Advanced framing techniques include increased stud spacing, which increases the fraction of wall covered by insulation rather than by wood, and the use of California or two-stud corners or other methods to improve insulation coverage at a structure's corners.

As opposed to a typical three-stud corner, a two-stud corner reduces lumber needs and lumber costs and permits the construction of a better-insulated corner. Drywall clips and stops support drywall at the corners and replace blocking at top plates, end walls, and corners. "It just makes economic sense," says Randy Nelson of Image Homes in Evergreen, Colo. A two-stud corner is faster to frame once the crew gets used to using drywall clips instead of screws and glue, and material costs are lower, he adds.

More information on advanced framing techniques can be found in two NAHB Research Center publications titled *Cost-Effective Home Building* and *Residential Construction Waste Management.*

Beyond the two-stud corner, many EVHA-winning builders increase exterior stud spacing to 24 inches on center to use less lumber and accommodate more insulation.

Another example of advanced framing is properly sized window headers that are insulated by sandwiching rigid insulation between the lumber.

Other techniques, such as using 2-inch-by-6-inch studs to create a deeper wall cavity, can increase a wall's overall R-value but are not considered advanced framing techniques.

Vernon McKown, president of sales for Ideal Homes of Norman, located in Norman, Okla., started learning about advanced framing techniques from a short course at the International Builders' Show. "We took the idea to our architect, who

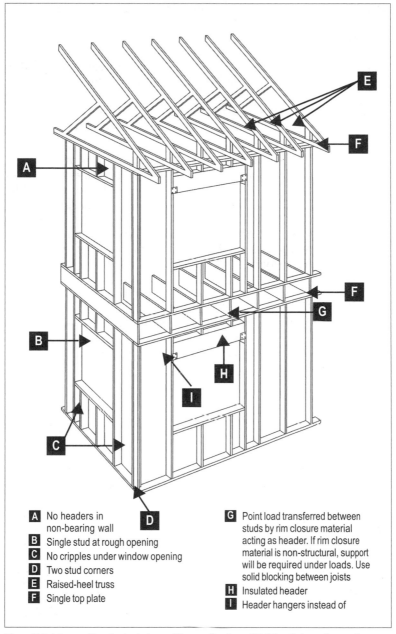

A No headers in non-bearing wall
B Single stud at rough opening
C No cripples under window opening
D Two stud corners
E Raised-heel truss
F Single top plate
G Point load transferred between studs by rim closure material acting as header. If rim closure material is non-structural, support will be required under loads. Use solid blocking between joists
H Insulated header
I Header hangers instead of

Figure 2.1 *Advanced framing techniques. Diagram Courtesy of Building Science Corporation.*

was familiar with the technique, and he drew up the plans," McKown says. "We simply call the techniques out in the scope of work because it is something different." McKown says that it is a no-cost item after the framers become familiar with the changes. Initially, he admits the technique slowed construction as framers learned the new process, but construction time was back to normal after framing a couple of houses. And according to McKown, the advanced framing did not cause any problems with local code officials because they were already familiar with the method.

McKown does not promote advanced framing in his marketing materials. He feels that there is a limit to the number of points to impress on customers, and framing is not one of the highest priorities. Mary Nelson of Image Homes disagrees. "The customers really understand, once we explain to them in layperson's terms, the reasons why our energy-efficient technologies work. It helps to show them individual features that add up to a lot of energy savings."

Structural Insulated Panels

For some builders, building a home with structural insulated panels (SIP) simplifies the process of creating an energy-efficient building envelope. SIPs are all-in-one building panels that combine two outer layers of oriented strand board (OSB) surrounding a rigid foam interior. When wall connections are sealed against air infiltration, SIPs can be used

Figure 2.2 *A worker cuts a SIP to size.*

Figure 2.3 *Window well in a double 2x4 wall.*

to create highly insulating walls, floors, and roofs.

Barbara Bannon Harwood of BBH Enterprises uses SIPs because of what she calls their "superior performance." Although she can build less expensively, she chooses to build with SIPs and other energy efficiency measures because it's what her customers want. According to Harwood, using SIPs adds about two percent to the wall cost over stick framing. Yet, as the price of lumber fluctuates and the quality of studs varies, builders can look to SIPs as an alternative framing system.

Harwood feels that a regular framing crew cannot necessarily install SIPs, which, according to Harwood, is contrary to what the manufacturers say. Harwood does not use SIPs in her affordable homes because it takes a little extra time and crew training. With custom homes it is easier to use SIPs because they have more time for construction and a larger construction budget, she says. In addition, some specialized equipment, such as a crane, may be needed to maneuver panels, especially if SIPs are used for the roof. When used as roofing panels, SIPs make it relatively easy to create vaulted ceilings up to 17 or 18 feet in height.

Figure 2.4 *Insulating Concrete Form foundation under construction.*

Insulating Concrete Forms

Insulating concrete forms (ICFs) are rigid plastic foam forms that hold concrete in place during curing and remain in place thereafter to serve as thermal insulation for concrete walls. The lightweight foam blocks, panels, or planks result in energy-efficient, durable walls. ICF material cost ranges from about $1.75 to about $3.50 per square foot in addition to installation labor, reinforcement, bracing, and concrete.

Tipp City, Ohio-based New Haven Construction used ICFs in its EVHA-winning homes because, according to Jeremy Tomb, ICFs provide a quiet, well-insulated wall assembly. Tomb also places a high value on long-lived materials that enhance security. "Although a little more expensive at the time of purchase, products that are more durable save on purchasing, labor, and disposal costs associated with replacing them, especially exterior materials."

Figure 2.5 *Insulating concrete form walls under construction.*

Double 2x4 Wall

Insulation of any thickness can be installed in a cavity between two walls. That is the concept behind Colorado Dream Homes' double wall system that features R-38 walls with fiberglass batt insulation. The

Figure 2.6 *Insulating concrete form house under construction.*

double wall system consists of two, 2x4 wall sections spaced 4 inches apart, creating a 12-inch wall cavity. This wall cavity is filled with R-38 batt insulation.

"Creating a double wall takes a little longer, but we save time by having detailed cut lists and panelizing many walls," says Tegan Brown for Pagosa Springs, Colo.-based Colorado Dream Homes. The double wall consumes floor space, but is part of the energy-efficient structure. Brown adds that the double wall creates a thick window sill that many buyers find attractive. In addition, the wall does not require any special skills or tools for design or construction—draftspersons create the cut lists and the regular framing crew assembles the wall.

Brown points out another feature of the double walls—the extra insulation keeps the interior space quieter while reducing utility bills. The double wall system sets Colorado Dream Homes apart from its competition. In fact, their customers are willing to pay the additional cost for thick walls, enhanced energy efficiency, and attractiveness.

Prefabricated Walls

Prefabricating wall panels in a factory or factory-like setting can offer several benefits over on-site building. A factory provides a worker-friendly environment with ready access to a wide array of precision and specialty tools and materials. Work stations tend to be conditioned and ergonomically designed for comfort, permitting workers to focus on what they are doing rather than on insects, weather, or other sources of discomfort. Quality control mechanisms can be implemented easily and improved workmanship promises a high-quality product at low cost. Waste recycling and reuse is made easy. Material costs are minimized and deliveries are simplified. Jobsite construction time and construction site waste are significantly reduced.

Figure 2.7 *A double wall system was used to create an R-38, fiberglass batt-insulation wall.*

DeLuca Enterprises of Newtown, Pa., uses prefabricated wood-frame walls with metal bracing. As Jim DeLuca says, "Our goal is to create a quality product that maximizes long-term value for the homeowner. The factory-made panels minimize construction defects. As a result, system efficiencies are improved."

Judy Fosdick of Tierra Concrete Homes in Pueblo, Colorado, builds

Figure 2.8 *A concrete panel that was poured around the perimeter is put into place by a crane.*

19

concrete wall panels on a mobile casting unit at the site, ships them by truck to the construction site, and lifts them into place via crane.

"It's a little more expensive—3 to 5 percent more with a custom home," says Fosdick. "But we're working on affordable homes that will yield an economy of scale we believe will eliminate the cost difference." Jobsite construction time is reduced significantly with prefabricated

Figure 2.9 *Prefabricated wall sections are assembled in the factory for shipment to the construction site.*

walls, Fosdick adds. It takes the firm about a day or two to assemble the prefabricated concrete walls on site as opposed to a week or more for completing conventional concrete construction. Fosdick claims that one benefit from factory-like methods of production is "that we don't need highly skilled workers. We often use migrant field workers—a step up for them and cost effective for us." Jobsite fabrication is substantially reduced. "Once the wall is raised, the rest of the work is just making connections."

Raised-Heel Roof Truss

Heat dissipation through the roof and walls makes up a significant portion of residential heat loss. But installing bulky insulation in the tight triangular corner where roof framing meets top plates can pose a problem. Often, insulation is simply squeezed into the space, reducing the material's R-value and allowing heat to escape at the roof edges. In cold climates, ice dams and structural damage can result.

Figure 2.10 *Raised-heel roof truss.*

Raised-heel trusses (also called energy trusses or oversized roof trusses) offer a solution by lifting the roof several inches to provide ample space above the top plate for installation of a thick layer of insulation. Alternatively, some builders simply lift the roof several inches by nailing a wide stud around the roof perimeter. Another option is to use a cantilevered truss, which is slightly oversized so that it becomes part of the overhang and creates additional space for insulation.

Dominion Building Group of Virginia Beach installs a uniform layer of insulation across the entire attic area of its homes by raising the roof as follows:

A specialized raised-heel roof truss is pentagonal in shape instead of the conventional triangular shape. The two vertical sides elevate the roof and allow installation of a thick, even layer of insualtion across the entire attic.

With raised-heel roof trusses, there are no additional labor costs for roof framing because the truss is simply a different shape and is installed in the same manner as standard roof trusses. However, there are additional siding costs.

- Roof rafters are attached atop a 2x12 board extending from the top plate
- A 2x12 raises the roof by 11 1/2 inches; and
- R-38 insulation is laid between the 2x12 ceiling joists.

The company's raised-roof design adds about $400 in material costs and five hours of labor, according to Andrew Joseph, vice president of Dominion Building Group. No design changes are required, but Joseph recommends deciding on the design before the plans are drawn in order to avoid confusion during plan review. The extra roof height requires additional siding and sheathing materials that need to be worked into the plans, and it is important to calculate any changes to the roof line caused by the added height, Joseph adds. Joseph also notes that making space for attic insulation does not require advanced skills or training. A carpenter or roofing contractor can perform the work.

Insulation

Insulation works like a blanket that helps keep houses warm. Properly installed insulation that completely fills wall cavities helps keep warmth indoors in the winter while gaps in the insulation allow heat to escape. Builders have many options for insulation products that blanket homes in warmth.

Batt Insulation

For many years, builders of energy-efficient homes have successfully used fiberglass batt insulation. To achieve higher-than-typical insulating values using fiberglass batt insulation, some builders use thicker wall construction, such as 2x6 framing members or a double-framed wall, to create a deeper cavity that can accommodate more batt insulation. Others use high-density batt insulation—or cover the outer wall with insulating sheathing—

Figure 2.11 *Certified contractor label.*

to boost wall R-values. When installed with care, batt insulation is a cost-effective way to create an energy-efficient house.

The NAHB Research Center recognizes that proper insulation installation is as important to

Figure 2.12 *Batt insulation.*

product performance as is the quality of the product itself. In response, the Research Center has developed the Trade Contractor Certification program for insulation and siding installation. Builders of energy-efficient homes can seek out insulation contractors that have passed the Research Center's third-party certification process.

To become a certified insulation installer, a trade contractor must pass an extensive audit. After certification, trade contractors are audited randomly twice each year to verify compliance. Audits include a series of detailed examinations of the contractor's quality control system and jobsite inspections. To learn more about the program or to find a certified contractor in your area, check out the NAHB Research Center Web site at www.nahbrc.org or call 800-638-8556.

Cellulose Insulation

When it's time to choose insulation, R-value is an important consideration, but it's not the only one. Other considerations include ease of installation, cost, resistance to air infiltration, and

contractor familiarity with the product. Cellulose insulation combines a higher R-value per inch of thickness (compared to fiberglass batt insulation) with some resistance to air infiltration. It is made from post-consumer recycled newspaper and newsprint waste from printing presses. Cellulose insulation is treated with a fire retardant, which also functions as an insecticide.

Figure 2.13 *Workers spray cellulose insulation into a wall cavity.*

Cellulose insulation comes in loose-fill or wall-spray form. Loose-fill cellulose insulation is either blown into a drywall-enclosed wall cavity or placed into a wall cavity by using a retainer system. The cellulose is then packed down to the proper density to achieve the final R-value, which, according to the Cellulose Insulation Manufacturers Association (CIMA), is between R-3.55 and R-3.85 per inch. With a little training, any insulation contractor can apply loose-fill insulation. CIMA publishes installation guidelines as well as charts that show the proper amount of insulation for various applications.

Wall-spray (also called wet-spray or damp-spray) cellulose insulation is spray-applied to a wall cavity with the use of special equipment. When sprayed, the insulation is combined with moisture to activate an adhesive that causes the insulation to stick to the wall cavity without a retainer system. Wall-spray cellulose has the same R-value as loose-fill insulation. Traditionally, the total cost to install wall-spray cellulose insulation is between 20 percent and 50 percent more than fiberglass batt insulation.

EVHA winner Gabriel Enterprises prefers wall-spray cellulose insulation in its energy-efficient houses. Jay Epstein, president, said he chose cellulose insulation for its resistance to air infiltration and to promote the use of recycled materials. Epstein attributes Gabriel homes' low air-infiltration rate to the use of cellulose insulation.

Epstein states that educating subcontractors is critical for ensuring customer satisfaction with wet-spray cellulose. He worked closely with his insulation contractor to ensure proper insulation placement. After the initial training, says Epstein, the cellulose installation requires no more effort than in the case of fiberglass batts. "The learning curve is steep at first, but after everyone is on board, the extra attention to detail does not cost any more overall," Epstein says.

Gary Michael

Figure 2.14 *Spray foam insulation.*

Spray Foam Insulation

Spray foam insulation combines insulation and air sealing in one step. Typical installation of fiberglass batt insulation leaves air gaps along the studs, at outlet boxes, and along electric wires. On extremely cold winter days, the homeowner may feel drafts near electrical outlets or see curtains move. Spray foam insulation suppresses drafts by filling wall cavities with solid foam. At an R-value of 3.6 per inch, foam insulation in a 2x 4 wall cavity is roughly equivalent to an R-13 batt. The foam also provides a barrier against air infiltration. Most spray foam insulation products do not contain ozone depleting hydrochlorofluorocarbons or off-gas any VOCs.

According to Harwood of BBH Enterprises, spray foam insulation costs about four times as much as traditional batt insulation per square foot. However, when combined with the steps to ensure a home's tightness, spray foam insulation is more competitive with batt insulation.

"Using Icynene [a brand of spray foam insulation] is easy," says Harwood. She uses contractors who have the necessary equipment and have been certified by the manufacturer. "It goes up faster than batts because it is simply sprayed on, and then expands outward to fill the wall cavity," Harwood says. "It takes some experience to spray the right amount. If you put too much on there can be a lot of waste. When applied by an experienced contractor, though, there is very little waste."

Harwood likes the air-infiltration barrier provided by spray foam as well as the material's sound-proofing properties. She uses it in garage walls to create an air barrier between the inside of the house and the garage in order to guard against infiltration of carbon monoxide. "It's an integral part of my indoor air quality package," she adds.

Insulating Sheathing

Many EVHA builders choose to use a layer of foam sheathing on the outside of their houses to provide continuous insulation around the homes. They specify the sheathing to cover uninsulated areas of a home—called thermal bridges—that can be a source of heat loss. Thermal bridges can include uninsulated studs, headers, and all-wood corners. Insulating sheathing can reduce the effects of thermal bridging by covering part or all of the entire outer shell of a home with foam insulation board.

Figure 2.15 *Insulating sheathing.*

The primary benefit of insulating sheathing is that it covers an entire wall without thermal breaks at studs. The disadvantage is that the wall is not as strong as a wall built with structural sheathing. Because foam insulation board does not provide racking resistance, provisions must be made to strengthen the structure and to meet building codes. Walls in which insulating sheathing replaces structural sheathing can meet building codes depending on the number of stories, the location of the house, and the methods used for adding structural strength. Some builders use structural sheathing at the building corners while others use let-in bracing.

Texas-based Newmark Homes uses a thin structural sheathing made from composite materials. The sheathing is applied at the building corners to achieve needed structural strength while still accommodating insulating sheathing at corners. Mike Beckett, executive vice president, points out that "when you add up all the areas without exterior wall insulation [when a builder uses structural sheathing at the corners], it can be 30 to 40 percent of the building surface area. It makes a big difference [to cover the structural sheathing with foam], especially if you aren't counting that into your air-conditioning load calculations."

Radiant Barrier Roof Sheathing

Because most solar heat gain is realized through the roof, attics tend to get extremely hot in warm, sunny climates. As the sun heats up a roof, conduction moves the heat to the inside of the sheathing, and the heat blasts into the attic by convection and radiation.

R-value only measures conduction heat transfer—radiation is not an integral part of that

> The added cost of radiant barriers makes more sense in hot climates. In other climates, look at the summer electric utility rates. If the local rate is higher than the national average, then the addition of a radiant barrier may be attractive for your home buyers.

number. However, radiant heat transfer is significant in an attic. Radiant barriers can block radiant heat transfer into the attic, reduce the overall attic temperature, and save on air-conditioning bills. The Florida Solar Energy Center claims that barriers "both save money and increase comfort" by blocking thermal radiation. A radiant barrier consists of a very thin layer of aluminum foil that is usually bonded to a plastic film or paper substrate. As use of radiant barriers has evolved, builders often opt for roof decking (plywood or OSB) laminated with a radiant barrier to ease the installation process. Radiant barriers must have a ventilated air space on the shiny side, and it is usually best to place the shiny side down to minimize dust build-up.

John M. Friesenhahn of Medallion Homes says, "In a hot climate, it's wonderful. It's easy to install—just put the shiny side down and nail it." Friesenhahn finds that the cost of laminated radiant barrier roof sheathing fluctuates with OSB pricing but is generally about 10 percent to 15 percent more than standard OSB sheathing. He shows off his attic space to prospective customers who then quickly recognize the comfort benefits. According to Friesenhahn, many customers note that they can even use the attic for storage. Because of Medallion's use of the material, Friesenhahn notes his competition now installs radiant barrier roof sheathing.

There is one disadvantage to using radiant barrier roof sheathing, Friesenhahn says. "All of the subcontractors in the area would come over to our house [while under construction] to eat lunch because it was noticeably cooler. It led to having to discard lots of trash that we didn't anticipate."

Frost-Protected Shallow Foundations

Figure 2.16 *Frost-protected shallow foundation.*

Frost-protected shallow foundations (FPSF) offer builders a lower-cost opportunity to build a structurally sound foundation. By placing rigid foam insulation board around the outside of a foundation in a prescribed manner, builders can effectively raise the frost depth of the soil and significantly reduce excavation costs.

Frost-protected shallow foundation footings are placed about 12 to 16 inches below grade. Insulation boards at the outside edge of the foundation then extend from above grade to the top of the footer. Wing insulation extends horizontally from the top of the footer outward and extends even farther in colder climates. Wing insulation may be unnecessary in mild climates.

Although commonly used in slab-on-grade foundations, FPSF can also be used with stem wall, floating slab, and unvented crawl space foundations. The NAHB Research Center publication, *Design Guide for Frost-Protected Shallow Foundations*, offers foundation and insulation details.

Frost-protected shallow foundations are more cost effective in colder climates with deeper frost lines than in temperate climates and are usually not cost effective on rocky sites. In addition, the use of exterior foundation insulation may necessitate nonstandard exterior finish details. The training of the crews also adds to cost; therefore, it is beneficial to use local tradespersons already familiar with FPSFs.

Judy Fosdick of Tierra Concrete Homes insists "[FPSFs] saves on excavation costs, preserves site details, and saves homeowners money. The trade-off is in the time needed to install the insulation. We save in concrete materials, yet use more rigid insulation. A 1988 study by the NAHB Research Center showed a 15 to 21 percent cost savings with FPSFs over conventional foundations."

Fosdick adds, "Our building department had not heard of [FPSFs] when we first talked with them. In each of three counties, we had to go to the appeals board for approval. We finally received approval by using supporting documentation from the NAHB Research Center, our engineer's testimony, and our statement of purpose for using it."

Tierra Concrete Homes did not need to make any design changes to accommodate FPSF. Though Fosdick says, "We did have to emphasize the importance of proper installation to the crew—that the work they are doing is very important to the success of the project. In addition, I personally made sure that everyone, even the subcontractors, followed through appropriately." When Neimeyer found scattered insulation board moved by the plumbing subcontractor, she realized the importance of educating all her subcontractors, even those not directly involved. "He didn't realize it was there for a purpose and simply moved it out of his way."

Fosdick's advice to builders considering FPSFs is to "get reliable information on how, how much, and how to configure and run it by the building department early on in the process so they are educated before they see the final drawings."

Duct Design

Inefficient ductwork can account for up to 30 percent of a home's energy loss, particularly if leaky ducts are located in unconditioned space. Even when ducts are located within a conditioned space, leaking air from ductwork can potentially lead to unbalanced conditions and suboptimal operation of the HVAC system.

Good duct design needs proper

Figure 2.17 *Mastic used at joints prevents air leakage from ducts.*

28

sizing of trunk and branch lines, turning vanes inside 90-degree elbows, transition takeoffs for each supply branch, and minimizing the length of duct runs. Good duct installation means sealing ducts with mastic, using only ducted returns rather than panned floor joist or stud cavity returns, and installing return ducts or transfer grilles in bedrooms. The most energy-efficient duct plan eliminates ductwork from attics, exterior walls, crawl spaces, and unheated basements.

Figure 2.18 *Ductwork in unconditioned space should be well insulated.*

Older houses were built "to breathe" and had less insulation than today's typical construction. (In other words, they were leaky.) Today's homes have more insulation and are more tightly constructed such that ductwork can be downsized. Good supply and return placement is still important, and HVAC professionals should use Air Conditioning Contractors of America's *Manuals T and D* to design duct systems.

"It may take effort to find contractors willing to do the calculations and redesign systems for optimal performance," says Richard Collier of R.E. Collier-Builder of Richmond. "But we were lucky. Our HVAC contractor attended a seminar in Richmond with us. We also worked with a consultant."

Collier adds that some of the framing in his homes required redesign to accommodate the new duct design. In the beginning, the redesign

Figure 2.19 *Insulation is attached to the rafters in this Las Vegas-area house featuring an unvented roof design.*

slowed construction as framers and HVAC contractors worked through the learning curve. But after a short time, the construction time returned to normal, he adds.

Collier feels that the redesigned duct system adds value to his homes. He explains to buyers how much they can expect to save by specifying advanced duct design. He even backs up his claim with a savings guarantee. "Consumers understand the concepts, but they react when they realize it will affect their bottom line," Collier says.

A few simple design rules can help you reduce or eliminate energy lost to the outdoors through ductwork:

• Locate ducts in conditioned basements or crawl spaces, between floors, and between interior wall partitions. Avoid running ducts in attics, unfinished basements, or exterior wall cavities.

• Where necessary, locate ducts within dropped ceilings, dropped soffits, or unventilated, insulated attics.

• Centrally locate supply registers to reduce duct length, installation costs, and duct energy losses and to ensure adequately high supply temperatures at the register.

• Seal ducts with mastic.

• Where reasonable, provide adequate insulation for all ductwork, including plenums, boots, and return ducts.

A unique method for bringing ducts into the conditioned space in hot climates is by using an unvented roof. Dave Beck of Pulte Home Corp.–Las Vegas division was concerned about duct leakage and implemented a plan for properly sealing ducts and moving them to a central location. Working with the Building America program (see Partnerships for Energy Efficiency section), Beck started placing insulation at the roof level instead of at the ceiling level, thereby containing all ductwork in insulated space in the attic. While Beck had seen research results that suggested the approach would work well in the hot climate where his firm builds, local building codes did not allow the practice. He turned to Building America for consultation and was able to provide Las Vegas officials with data that convinced them to accept the design option.

Subcontractors need to be field trained in unvented roof design installation. "It's a different system,"Beck says. "But, once crews are trained, it's a minor change in practices." Beck believes that there is no incremental cost associated with unvented roof design. "Our entire energy package adds $300 or $400 to total house costs," he adds.

Window Selection

With all the window choices in today's market, it is hard to select the right window for a given application. The following sections can help clarify window technologies.

NFRC Rating

The National Fenestration Rating Council (NFRC) has developed a standardized system of ratings for windows. Ratings address U-factor and, for some products, the solar heat gain coefficient (SHGC) and visible transmittance. There are plans to include information about air infiltration.

Figure 2.20 *National Fenestration Rating Council label displayed on windows.*

U-Factor

U-factor, or the rate of heat conduction through a material, is the reciprocal of R-value. The lower the U-factor, the higher the window's resistance is to heat flow. U-factor can be enhanced by applying a low-E coating to the window glass, using an inert gas such as argon in the air space between two window panes, increasing the number of window panes, or improving the insulating ability of the frame, spacers, or sash. Adding a low-E coating and argon gas between window panes will decrease the U-factor of a double-pane window by about 40 percent. A lower U-factor means better energy performance.

Solar Heat Gain Coefficient

The SHGC is the fraction of solar radiation falling on a window that is transmitted through the glass as heat. The desirable SHGC may be high or low depending on the climate and window orientation.

31

Low-E Coating

Low-E (low-emissivity) coatings reflect heat. Depending on the placement of the coating, the glazing can help reduce winter heat loss, lower summer heat gain, or both. Low-E coatings can significantly improve a window's U-factor. The coatings are placed on different surfaces of the glass to achieve different effects. For example, a low-E coating applied to the outer surface of the inner pane of glass encourages passive solar gain while a coating applied to the inside of the exterior window pane is most effective in minimizing solar heat gain.

Not all low-E glass is right for all applications. Because low-E coatings affect both U-factor and the SHGC, choosing the right window can be tricky. In a passive solar home designed with properly sized overhangs, a high SHGC is desirable on south-facing windows. If a home is not designed with passive solar gain in mind, a low SHGC and low U-factor should be used on the south side. For east- and west-facing glass, a low SHGC is desirable to avoid solar heat gain when the sun is low in the sky as it sets and rises. For north-facing glass, a low U-factor is preferable.

Inert Gas–Filled Windows

An inert gas such as argon or krypton reduces the conduction of heat through the air space between two window panes as well as the overall transfer of heat through a window. Gas-filled windows are used primarily in climates where reducing heat loss is a priority.

Orlo Stitt of Stitt Energy Systems in Rogers, Ark., uses low-E windows throughout his homes. He also uses argon-filled windows but considers low-E coatings a high priority. Before Stitt specifies windows, however, he makes certain that they face the right direction. He avoids west- and north-facing windows but relies on south-facing windows to maximize solar heat gain during the heating season. According to Stitt, low-E, argon-filled windows cost about $20 to $25 more than their less-efficient counterparts.

Visible Transmittance

Visible transmittance (VT) refers to the fraction of visible sunlight that is transmitted through a window as light. High versus low VT indicates that an interior space will be brighter. Builders desiring to incorporate daylighting into their homes select a higher VT.

Air Infiltration Rate

The air infiltration rate is the rate at which air enters through cracks or gaps in the window assembly, thereby causing heat loss or gain. Air infiltration is tested at a specified pressure designed to induce infiltration. It is important to note that without additional air-sealing details, air can leak around the rough framing of windows and compromise the window system's efficiency, regardless of a window's rated air infiltration.

Lighting

Barbara Harwood of BBH Enterprises uses compact fluorescent lighting (CFL) throughout all of her homes. CFLs are miniature versions of traditional fluorescent lights that screw into a regular incandescent fixture. With carefully chosen light fixtures, the light from CFLs is not harsh. In fact, Harwood says it is possible to create the desired ambience. Harwood notes that in the past it was difficult to find fixtures that would accommodate CFLs. Now builders have lots of options. "People can't tell the difference. We showed one house to 5,000 people at the parade of homes and nobody thought the lighting was any different. Different shades of lighting are now available so that the (CFL) light looks more like incandescent lamps."

Harwood even uses compact fluorescent lamps in indirect lighting fixtures. She orders small CFLs from a company in Dallas and used 50 of the low-wattage bulbs in one indirect fixture. "It was a

Figure 2.21 *These fluorescent lighting fixtures use one-quarter the electricity of incandescent bulbs and do not emit nearly as much heat.*

little more difficult than your typical lighting application," she admits. It cost $350 for the single fixture—the lamps cost $2.65 each and then needed the addition of clamps and a transformer on each end.

Harwood claims that it is not difficult to specify CFLs throughout a home. "Just call your lighting supplier and tell them you want to specify all CFLs in your home." After suppliers perform the work once, they are sufficiently skilled to call themselves experts, she adds.

Compact fluorescent lamps are not inexpensive. High-efficiency, swirl-type CFLs cost about $18 each while standard CFLs, which produce about four times as much light per watt than incandescent bulbs, cost about $13 to $15 each. The trade-off is all types of CFLs will last for thousands of hours; therefore, the lifetime price of a CFL is less expensive than incandescent lamps. The savings are even greater if you include the reduced electricity bills.

Heating, Ventilating, and Air Conditioning

Sealed-Combustion Appliances

Sealed-combustion appliances should be specified in tightly constructed homes when gas or oil appliances are used. As energy-efficient buildings become tighter, concern increases over carbon monoxide produced by a home's combustion appliances. Conventional combustion appliances use indoor air for combustion, with the air ultimately supplied by air infiltration. This usually works well, but in a tight home or under unusual conditions, combustion air can be drawn down the flue and releases combustion products into the home in a process known as backdrafting.

Sealed-combustion appliances, including furnaces, water heaters, gas fireplaces, and some ovens, rely on a pipe and power vent to bring outside air directly to the burner. Exhaust flue gases (combustion products) are in turn vented directly to the outside without a draft hood or damper. Sealed-combustion appliances generally operate more efficiently than atmospherically vented appliances and pose less risk of introducing dangerous combustion gases into the house.

Sealed-combustion appliances have a longer expected life span than their conventional counterparts because they produce less damaging by-products from incomplete combustion, such as soot that can clog burners and generally reduce appliance life. "We always put a high value on materials that have extended life spans. We install versatile sealed-combustion, condensing-gas furnaces that use 100 percent outdoor air for combustion," says Jeremy Tomb of New Haven Construction in Tipp City, Ohio. "We not only define economical as the bottom price on a home but have also expanded our definition to include the cost of operation and maintenance for our homes."

Sometimes the lower cost of installing a venting system for a condensing furnace can offset the additional cost of higher efficiency equipment. A conventional gas furnace requires a sheet metal flue routed vertically through the house while a sealed combustion furnace requires only a polyvinyl chloride (PVC) vent that can be routed horizontally. A PVC vent is often much simpler to install than a sheet metal flue pipe.

The most efficient sealed-combustion appliances are the condensing types, and the highest-efficiency gas furnace on the market today has an Annual Fuel Utilization Efficiency (AFUE) of 96.6 percent. In other words, 96.6 percent of the fuel is converted to useful heat. High-efficiency furnaces recover heat from exhaust gases and send less heat up the flue. Water that condenses out of the low-temperature exhaust must be drained. Builders should expect to pay about $200 more for a sealed combustion furnace over a conventional furnace. The *Consumer Guide to Home Energy Savings* (see Resources) includes an updated list of the most energy-efficient heating systems and water heaters on the market.

High-Efficiency Cooling Systems

Most new homes today are equipped with mechanical cooling and some electric utilities even subsidize the cost of high-efficiency equipment. Despite the equipment's energy-efficient operation and subsidized market promotions, many consumers choose not to select high-efficiency systems because of higher initial cost or a bad experience with improperly sized systems. Builders can, however, promote the use of energy-efficient cooling systems by selecting high-efficiency equipment, following industry standard methods for systems sizing, and tightly sealing and efficiently designing ductwork.

To size an HVAC system properly, a builder or subcontractor should follow an industry-approved sizing standard such as *Manual J: Residential Load Calculation* by the Air Conditioning Contractors of America, *Cooling and Heating Load Calculation Manual, GRP 138* by the American Society of Heating, Refrigerating, and Air-Conditioning Engineers, or *Heat Loss Calculation Guide No. H-22* by the Hydronics Institute.

35

Several technologies can improve the energy efficiency of cooling systems. While most heat pumps and air conditioners use a single-speed compressor that runs at full speed regardless of heating or cooling needs, some newer units employ variable speed compressors that run at the capacity appropriate for satisfying the cooling demand. Other systems use variable-speed fans for air distribution that move only as much air as necessary in order to maintain comfort levels and maximize electrical savings.

By properly sizing cooling systems, builders can avoid many consumer complaints and callbacks. Rule-of-thumb sizing procedures and generic charts should not be used. Oversized equipment is costly and inefficient and has poor dehumidification capabilities. Poor dehumidification occurs because oversized equipment cools the air quickly and does not run long enough to dehumidify. Oversized systems cycle frequently, thereby increasing the likelihood of failures and requiring more frequent maintenance. Undersized systems will not adequately cool a house during peak demand.

Sealing ductwork with mastic is another method for enhancing energy efficiency in cooling systems. Leaky ducts cause electrical resistance or back-up heat to operate more frequently than necessary in heat pumps and drastically reduce the efficient operation and comfort of air-conditioning units. Studies performed in Florida found that duct leaks can account for up to 25 percent of a home's heating and cooling load. Do not use temporary fixes such as duct tape to seal ductwork—instead, use water-based mastics that offer non-toxic, effective air sealing.

Figure 2.22 *A vertical bore hole is dug for a geothermal loop by using well-drilling equipment.*

Figure 2.23 *Workers making the loop connection to the house.*

Figure 2.24 *Interior geothermal equipment.*

Geothermal Heating and Cooling Systems

Douglas Holdridge of Holdridge Homes in Perrysburg, Ohio, hit a few bumps on the road installing geothermal systems in his homes. His subcontractors were not willing to run load calculations or seal ductwork, essential aspects of installing a geothermal system. In addition, he found that most companies were familiar with standard ductwork and sizing but unfamiliar with geothermal systems. Because Holdridge wanted to provide his customers with energy-efficient, comfortable homes, he persevered and then learned about geothermal systems himself. "We made a lot of mistakes along the way," says Holdridge, "but we learned by doing. Also, the local utility ran blower door tests and the manufacturer provided some technical support."

Other sources of support include the Geothermal Heat Pump Consortium, a Washington, D.C.-based industry group that provides training and maintains a list of manufacturers, and the International Ground Source Heat Pump Association, which offers training courses and maintains a fairly extensive list of qualified installers. Another geothermal builder, McNaughton Homes of Pa., looked to the expertise of manufacturers and the local utility company's Comfort Home Program to learn how to seal the building envelope and cut down drafts.

> **G**eothermal systems are more energy efficient and deliver heated air at a higher temperature than air-source heat pumps. Rather than using outdoor air that is subject to large fluctuations in temperature, geothermal systems draw heat from below the earth's surface to take advantage of stable temperatures.

Geothermal systems have two basic components—the outside ground loop and the indoor equipment. There is no outdoor compressor as with traditional air-conditioning systems. According to the Geothermal Heat Pump Consortium, systems cost between $2,000 and $5,000 more than conventional HVAC systems. The advantage lies in the monthly cost savings.

To minimize the size (and the initial cost) of the geothermal system, Holdridge ensures that his homes start out energy efficient. He specifies highly efficient windows, 2x6 framing with cellulose insulation, extensive air sealing, sealed ductwork, energy-efficient appliances, and a heat recovery ventilator.

Installing geothermal systems does not change the sequence or timing of construction, but it does require a little more work upfront. As with any heating system, proper design, particularly of ductwork and equipment, is crucial. Holdridge performs the heat load, duct sizing, and ground loop sizing calculations himself. Although an experienced contractor or possibly a local utility could complete the calculations, Holdridge prefers to retain control over the entire process. Though geothermal installations are becoming more common and as a result, more HVAC contractors are growing familiar with them. Mark McNaughton of McNaughton Homes relies on experienced HVAC contractors and the local utility for sizing systems. "They run the calculations based on the industry standards," he says.

> *Because the upfront cost of a geothermal system is higher than conventional HVAC systems, it doesn't make sense to install geothermal in a house that is not efficient to begin with.*
>
> *– Douglas Holdridge,* Holdridge Homes

Geothermal systems work for all homes, from affordable to luxury units. "The systems have been a great seller in areas where gas is unavailable," Holdridge says, "because customers understand the utility bill very well." McNaughton agrees, saying many "people understand the benefits; the systems are an easy sell." Although a good geothermal system costs about double that of a standard air-source heat pump, it provides higher delivery air temperatures, more comfort, and lower energy bills. "I sell comfort and low maintenance," says McNaughton.

Solar Water Heating

Harnessing energy from the sun to heat water is nothing new—solar water heaters have been commercially available since the 1800s. What is new is how solar water heaters look. Most modern solar water heaters mount flush with a home's roof and resemble skylights. Solar water heating is an environmentally sound way to reduce energy bills, and several buyers of EVHA-winning houses have reaped the benefits of solar water heating.

"It can cut energy bills in half," says Orlo Stitt of Stitt Energy Systems, "because, when you create a super energy-efficient building, water heating becomes a much more significant portion of the utility bill."

Stitt offers solar hot water as an option in all his homes. He states that it usually takes a measure of persuasion to convince the customer to buy the system. Many buyers balk at the $3,760 price, which covers a 4-foot-by-10-foot solar panel operated by photovoltaic power and a 105-gallon storage tank.

Yet in Arkansas, where Stitt builds, the system can supply the entire hot water load for a family of four for about eight months of the year. "You can certainly get hot water on overcast days, just like you can get a sunburn. But first, you should minimize hot water loads by using water-efficient appliances." A manually operated electric element provides back-up heat during the months when solar water heating cannot meet the entire load or when guests are visiting. "Of course," Stitt adds, "teenagers use a lot of hot water, so the system might pro-

Figure 2.25 *This 4-foot-by-10-foot hot water panel can supply a family of four with 75 percent of its water heating needs, and the pump is powered by photovoltaic solar energy (see small photovoltaic panel at left).*

vide a little less of the load in that case." Even so, the cost benefit is the same no matter how much hot water is used.

Stitt Energy Systems mounts its solar hot water systems flush with the roof. According to Stitt, customers don't like the old "spider mount" style in which panels were mounted on poles to provide optimal orientation and efficiency. "Panels don't have to be placed at the optimal angle because what you gain in efficiency, you lose in customer satisfaction," says Stitt. "You may need to increase panel area [with a flush-mount system], but customers will like it." Stitt Energy designs its homes with the intent of placing solar panels on top of the roof optimizing the efficiency of flush-mount solar collectors.

High-Efficiency Appliances

When selecting appliances, Stitt always looks for both the ENERGY STAR logo and the yellow EnergyGuide label. "It's the easiest way to find energy-efficient appliances," he says. Stitt also looks at water consumption because the amount of water used by an appliance also affects energy use. However, the presence of an EnergyGuide label does not indicate energy efficiency—all major appliances must be sold with the EnergyGuide label. "The labels can sometimes be tricky," Stitt warns.

Figure 5.7 *An ENERGY STAR logo.*

He points out that EnergyGuide labels compare horizontal-axis washing machines (European-style machines that tumble rather than agitate clothes) with other horizontal-axis machines. "The scale is different [than that for conventional machines], and the label makes horizontal-axis machines look much less efficient than they are."

The initial cost of energy-efficient appliances usually exceeds that of conventional appliances, but the lifetime cost of energy-efficient appliances is lower. Many pay back their premium cost in a short period through utility cost savings.

Horizontal-axis washing machines cost $600 and up. Super-efficient dishwashers can cost $250 more than other premium dishwashers. They use approximately 4.1 gallons per full cycle and 60 percent less energy than conventional machines. The biggest selling point, Stitt says, is their quiet operation.

In addition, Stitt does not recommend using side-by-side refrigerators, icemakers, or chilled water service, all features that reduce overall energy efficiency. Energy-efficient refrigerators usually cost more, but

Figure 2.27 *This refrigerator and dishwasher have EnergyGuide labels clearly displayed. Customers walking through this model home can see the difference in the builder's appliances.*

forgoing features such as icemakers can reduce their cost.

Stitt also recommends visiting other home building shows to see the latest products or obtaining information on ENERGY STAR appliances from the ENERGY STAR appliance Web site (www.energystar.gov).

Heat Recovery Ventilation

Energy-efficient homes are not drafty, but very tight construction can compromise IAQ if outdoor air is not intentionally brought into the home. Therefore, homes that are particularly tight often use mechanical ventilation to introduce fresh air into the

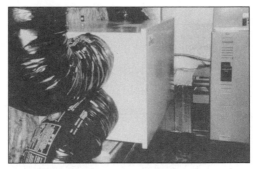

Figure 2.28 *Heat recovery ventilation system.*

house. The problem is ventilation undermines a home's energy efficiency by exhausting conditioned air and replacing it with outdoor air.

Heat recovery ventilators (HRVs) are absolutely worth the approximately $900 they add to construction costs, says Barbara Harwood of BBH Enterprises. HRVs maintain a low-velocity, constant flow of fresh air into a home while recapturing 70 percent to 80 percent of heat contained in exhaust air.

HRVs can be window- or wall-mounted or whole-house ducted systems. In some cases, ductwork for a central heating and cooling system can also provide airflow to the HRV. However, HRVs are usually ducted separately from the HVAC system. BBH Enterprises uses dedicated ducting for HRV systems, placing intake and exhaust vents on opposite sides of the house. "You have to duct it properly," Harwood says. "You can't place an intake vent right next to a fireplace, for example."

Even though she has used the same contractor for several years, Harwood is seeking a new contractor outside her market and is surprised by the large number of contractors experienced with mechanical ventilation systems. She recommends the development of a highly specific request for proposals to ensure that contractors perform the required calculations and design the systems according to industry recommendations.

Chapter Three

Energy- and Resource-Efficient Construction

Energy and resource efficiency begins with a carefully planned house design but is not complete until the plans are properly executed during the construction process. Carrying out design details to specifications helps ensure that a house will meet builder and customer expectations.

Plans are carried out by trade contractors, who are the most important allies in energy-efficient construction. It is very important to work with trade contractors so that design plans are properly implemented.

Working with Trade Contractors

Sometimes a significant hurdle to energy-efficient construction is trade contractor buy-in. Trade contractors may not be familiar with some efficiency techniques and need to be field-trained. Other techniques require few, if any, changes in practice.

To overcome this hurdle, Perry Bigelow, president of Bigelow Group of Palatine, Ill., organizes team meetings in the field with subcontractors. The company looks at a particular design issue, determines who is responsible for getting the job done most effectively, and then brings all the appropriate people together in the field to hash out construction issues. Bigelow realizes that subcontractors know the most about how a job gets done and that their input is crucial to smooth operation. "The meetings are always fun and high energy," Bigelow says, "and they generate a lot of great ideas and creative solutions. The subs appreciate that we value their opinions because, after all, they are the professionals."

Charlie Scott of Carmel, Ind.-based Estridge Companies says that he has had no problem with trade contractors installing efficient features. "We just give them the plans, and that's the way they do it." Scott improves his relationship with trade contractors by tying payments to quality, budget, and schedule. He offers trade contractors cash bonuses for finding ways to save time or materials. "We've built loyalty with our trade contractors [through these programs]," Scott says. "And we save money and improve our processes by getting input from the people who are doing the job." For more information about bonus incentives for trade contractors, call the NAHB Research Center's ToolBase Hotline at 800-898-2842.

The Estridge Companies of Indiana builds 500 homes a year and is a 1998 Gold Winner of the National Housing Quality Award and the EnergyValue Housing Award. The firm's cash incentive program for subcontractors who save materials, keep on schedule, and build a quality home is just one aspect of the high-quality construction practices that help Estridge save money and win customers.

EVHA-winning builders say it usually takes a little extra time, detailed plans, and maybe a little training or encouragement to get trade contractors to change their practices. However, the result is a high-quality product that satisfies customers.

Implementing Energy Efficiency in Production Homes

NVR (Ryan Homes) of Thurmont, Md., builds more than 10,000 homes per year. When it comes to implementing energy efficient practices, NVR does it in a big way. With its standard energy package (SEP) that includes air sealing and using the appropriate amount of insulation, NVR provides its customers with a tight, energy-efficient house. As a result, Larry Bassett of NVR states that many customers are pleasantly surprised by the level of cost savings they achieve.

Because NVR is so large, it benefits from in-house engineers and architects who determine the most cost-effective energy practices, a cadre of field supervisors who ensure that subcontractors put the measures into place correctly, and a production plant in which air barriers are installed on wall panels under controlled conditions. The company's sheer size also ensures that efficiency measures make an impact on the energy consumption of the new housing stock.

In developing its SEP, NVR underwent a long process of trial and error. Bassett recommends that builders interested in increasing their homes' energy efficiency look first at what other builders are doing. By doing your homework you will shorten the learning curve, but once the techniques are learned, the SEP does not change NVR's construction schedule, Bassett says. "It is an integral part of every phase of construction, so it is automatically implemented."

Figure 3.1 *This prototype house by NVR Homes proved that production builders can cost effectively implement energy-and resource-efficient measures. NVR Homes puts a standard energy package in all of its homes.*

Throughout the company's production training program, field supervisors learn about the techniques involved in the SEP. In turn, supervisors train trade contractors in the field. To ensure that all procedures are properly executed, subcontractors are not paid until they complete a checklist, signed by the field supervisor, that states that the SEP requirements were satisfied per specification. As further incentive, the bonus program for field supervisors is tied into the SEP's implementation.

Bassett thinks that today's home buyers are keenly aware of basic home building practices and that a system like the SEP appeals to them. The utility cost savings are highly marketable and NVR makes energy features apparent to home buyers. Features such as air sealing and high levels of insulation are easy for customers to understand, he says.

Figure 3.2 *Air sealing around window openings.*

Air Sealing

Button up against the cold! is a phrase familiar to school kids scurrying out the door. Builders can learn a valuable lesson from their youth—buttoning up houses reduces air infiltration into (or out of) a house and dramatically increases energy efficiency. By using sealing materials such as gaskets, foam, and caulk, builders can cut down infiltration and dramatically reduce energy losses.

Air-sealing techniques include sealing at the sill plate and top plate (usually with a gasket material), around the rim joist and window and door openings, and at all penetrations (such as electrical outlets or plumbing holes) through exterior walls or between conditioned and unconditioned spaces. An air-sealing package can also include a properly installed air barrier with taped seams.

Air sealing is a large part of building an energy-efficient home. Provisions must be made so that an adequate amount of fresh air reaches the occupants. Mechanical ventilation is often added to ensure an adequate supply of fresh air.

Figure 3.3 *Rim joist detailing.*

Air sealing a typical home, not including housewrap, costs about $400 to $500.

Many builders tend to rely on a single contractor to do most air sealing, thereby ensuring a consistent and efficient job. For larger builders, the sealing contractor can be a full-time employee whose job is exclusively air sealing. Other companies rely on their insulation contractors.

Mechanical ventilation is advised in tightly sealed homes in order to replace stale air with fresh outdoor air to eliminate concerns about IAQ. Many en-

Figure 3.4 *Air sealing around window openings.*

ergy-efficient builders install
heat recovery (or energy recovery) ventilators (HRVs)
that recover heat from outgoing, conditioned air to provide
energy-efficient ventilation
(see Heat Recovery Ventilation section).

Figure 3.5 *Air sealing ductwork penetrations between conditioned and unconditioned space.*

Airtight Drywall Approach

Builders of energy-efficient, durable projects trying to create tight homes might turn to their drywall installers for help.
Drywall, a component of most new homes, provides an excellent
barrier against airflow. The airtight drywall approach is a
method for installing drywall that limits air infiltration by using adhesive, caulk, foam, or gaskets to create a seal along top
and bottom plates on exterior walls; around rough openings; at
top plates of interior walls adjacent to unconditioned spaces; at
the first stud in an interior wall; and along the inside of the top
and bottom of first stud on an interior wall partition. Special
electrical boxes provide continuous air sealing. The approach
seals all points where air could flow through a wall and does not
rely on a vapor barrier or additional air barrier.

> *[The airtight drywall approach] was our key to being able to switch from building very energy-efficient custom homes to building equally efficient affordable homes at the production level.*
>
> *– Perry Bigelow, Bigelow Group*

"We use the air-
tight drywall approach
on all our homes,"
Bigelow of Bigelow
Group says. "It was our
key to being able to
switch from building
very energy-efficient
custom homes to build-
ing equally efficient af-
fordable homes at the production level." By combining the airtight drywall approach with other energy-efficiency measures,
Bigelow can guarantee that the annual heating bills on his Chi-
cago-area homes remain under $400.

Bigelow decided to use the system after he experienced diffi-
culty in using polyethylene as an effective airflow barrier. "Once
the drywall is up, we didn't know if the drywall person had vio-
lated the air barrier,"Bigelow says. "It is impractical to have some-

one overseeing the drywall installation." Bigelow says that it was easy to start implementing the approach. He simply designed and specified the plans and then showed the crews how to get started in the field.

To ensure that drywall sealing is performed exactly as specified, Bigelow relies on a staff person who does most of the air sealing work on the 150 homes the firm builds each year. According to Bigelow, it takes the person between one and a half to two days to complete the work, depending on the house size. "I don't know what the cost is [compared to conventional practice] because it's the only way we do the work." With a couple of exceptions (e.g., the carpenters glue the subfloor to the band joist and the drywallers seal around windows by installing a J-channel), most of the sealing work is done just before drywall installation.

Bigelow strongly advises anybody building a tight, energy-efficient house to be aware of the relationship between IAQ and carbon monoxide. Mechanical ventilation and sealed combustion appliances can help prevent any IAQ problems.

Insulating and Sealing Ductwork

Homeowners interested in reducing monthly energy costs typically consider increasing insulation levels or upgrading windows. What often goes unnoticed, however, is uninsulated ductwork located in attics, garage ceilings, and crawl spaces. In fact, placing ducts in unconditioned spaces is much like putting them outdoors, or worse. For example, an air-conditioning duct in a hot attic might perform even less efficiently than if it were located out-

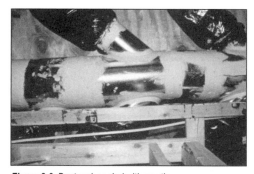

Figure 3.6 *Ductwork sealed with mastic.*

side, because an attic is almost always warmer than the outdoors during the cooling season. The most energy-efficient buildings have sealed ductwork in the conditioned space.

Still, if ductwork has to be run through unconditioned space, all ductwork should be carefully airsealed with mastic and then

insulated. Conventionally installed ductwork located in unconditioned space can lead to pressure imbalances, thermal losses,
and moisture problems. Research indicates that average energy-
related duct losses run between 20 percent and 35 percent.

Waste Management

Waste management involves several tasks that add up to
savings for builders and less solid waste in our landfills. Man-
aging waste includes reducing jobsite waste and the volume of
materials used for construction, using recycled-content products,
and making it easy for homeowners to minimize waste. In short,
it is a big job that can reap big rewards.

Jobsite Waste Reduction

Reducing jobsite waste cuts down on handling time, transportation costs, and tipping fees and, hence, saves a builder money
and time. In addition, waste reduction can actually increase energy and resource efficiency.

According to the *Residential Construction Waste Management
Guide* (see Resources), between 60 percent and 80 percent of
jobsite waste takes the form of wood, drywall, and cardboard.
Scrap wood can be minimized by using advanced framing techniques in which a building is designed at 2-foot increments to
limit scrap (see Figure 2.1). Cardboard recycling is usually cost
effective, especially when cost is based on volume. Although
manufacturers are looking into drywall recycling and drywall
scraps can be used in some agricultural applications, drywall is
currently difficult to recycle. Other waste such as metal and vi-
nyl has good market value but is generally produced in such low
volumes on a jobsite that recycling does not make economic
sense for most builders. While economics of recycling generally
depend on the local market, a builder or group of builders might
be able to create enough demand to change the local recycling
market.

Good planning is the best way to reduce jobsite waste, says
Charlie Scott of the Estridge Companies His company performs
its own takeoffs and provides the lumber supplier with a detailed lumber list. "That's our biggest contributor [to waste re-
duction]," says Scott. "We count every piece of lumber that
should go into a house, and we make sure that is what is delivered to the jobsite."

As incentive to the framing crew for saving materials, the money saved from lumber returned to the supplier is passed on to the crew. "It's amazing how they find ways to save lumber," Scott says. Framers take the toe boards they use on the roof to the next job site. The lumber cash incentives do not last forever, however. After a period of time, the company readjusts its purchasing to reflect the actual amount of lumber needed for a particular design. But, Scott adds, the framers help us in the long run, and we save hundreds of dollars per house on the framing materials alone.

> **C**harlie Scott of the Estridge Companies offers a three-step waste reduction program:
> - Do your own detailed estimates of materials.
> - Check material once it arrives on the jobsite.
> - Share savings with your partner/ subcontractor.

For more information about jobsite waste reduction, visit the NAHB Research Center Web site at www.nahbrc.org.

Recycled-Content Building Materials

Not only does the process of home building create waste, but industries that manufacture building products also dispose of waste. Using recycled-content building materials can help reduce building industry waste overall. Examples of recycled building materials include several types of insulation, recycled-content asphalt shingles, carpet and carpet pads, concrete with flyash recycled from power plants, and specialty products such as recycled-content glass tile and window frames or recycled plastic lumber decking and countertops. The use of engineered wood products has reduced reliance on high-quality resources such as old-growth trees. For example, OSB is made from young, fast-growing "scrub" trees and finger-jointed studs allow small trees to be made into long studs.

Panelized Wall Construction

DeLuca Enterprises of Newtown, Pa. operates a panelization plant that manufactures wall sections for all DeLuca homes. The company, which builds 250 homes per year, uses factory panelization to control quality and waste. According to Perry DeSiato, vice president, "Factory panelization minimizes construction defects that could affect system efficiency and thermal loss. Every part of the wall, including the insulating sheathing, is put together under controlled conditions. Waste is minimized through factory controls and in-plant recycling."

Reducing In-Home Waste

Builders generate waste during the construction of a house. Homeowners, in turn, continue to create waste during the life of the home. Recycling centers in the home permit homeowners to cutback on their solid waste production. In-counter compost bins make it easy and unobtrusive for homeowners to recycle food scraps into usable garden compost.

Education is a key component to homeowner waste reduction. To enable recycling, some builders include local recycling phone numbers and collection information in homeowner manuals.

Chapter Four

Cutting-Edge Technologies

Photovoltaic Roofing Products

For years, people have wanted to realize the cost-benefits of solar energy without seeing solar energy components on their roofs. Although the term "solar power" may be synonymous with energy efficiency and environmental friendliness, solar power has been unpopular in part because it involves an unattractive structure. In response, manufacturers have developed building-integrated photovoltaic (BIPV) systems that are incorporated into roofing materials. The result is an unobtrusive solar power system that is installed with the roofing material.

Figure 4.1 *Workers install a photovoltaic shingle roofing product. The product installs just like asphalt shingles.*

BIPV products include electricity-generating shingles that resemble asphalt shingles, standing-seam metal roofing, and slate or concrete tiles. Most residential BIPV systems consist of a photovoltaic (PV) building material that produces electrical current, batteries that store energy, and an inverter that converts photovoltaic current (DC, or direct current) to standard household current (AC, or alternating current). In some instances, batteries are eliminated such that the utility company serves as the storage and back-up power supplier. Some states have enacted net metering laws that require the utility company to pay the homeowner the same price at which the homeowner buys electricity from the supplier. Net metering causes the electric meter to run backward and improves the economic feasibility of PV systems.

EVHA winner Barbara Harwood of BBH Enterprises has used standing-seam metal PV roofing. According to Harwood, installing BIPV was "definitely an education." She specified a 960-watt array that was integrated into a standing-seam metal roof. The whole system cost about $10 per watt installed, or $9,600 in total. Harwood received a $5,000 grant from TU Electric, the local E Seal-certified utility, which brought the cost to the home buyer below $5,000.

Harwood, who builds mainly with SIPs, applied the BIPV roof on top of the SIPs. At first, when the electrical contractor looked at the job, he said, "Look at this mess, how do we do this?" But, Harwood says, "We—electrician, builder, and solar manufacturer—scratched our heads together and figured it out." The main challenge was how to run the wires through the SIP roof panels. The solution was to run the wires along the ridge vent and in through the weatherhead.

Harwood faced a similar situation with the roofing installer. At first, the roofer eyed the standing-seam metal roof material with suspicion. After a little coaxing, the roofer realized that the product installs in the same manner as an ordinary standing-seam metal roof.

While BBH Enterprise's 960-watt system will not supply all the electricity needs of its homes, some PV systems can supply 100 percent of the electrical load. A whole-house solar electric power system needs to produce between 2,000 and 4,000 watts. Maximizing the efficiency of electric appliances makes economic sense when using solar-powered electricity to supply the entire house because the cost of increasing the capacity of the system almost always exceeds the cost of upgrading appliance efficiency.

Roofs with an integrated solar power system should face as close as possible to due south; efficiency declines as orientation deviates from true solar south. With the current expense of BIPV systems, a reduction in efficiency can be costly. PV roofing products and systems are currently available through distributors of solar energy products. There are customers who are willing to pay a premium for PV products. Like the customer who wants a high-end sink, some customers are willing to pay extra for a product such as PV that they see as a desirable feature.

Fuel Cells

In the future, builders may be able to put power plants in their homes. The fuel cell technology now under development could permit a dishwasher-sized fuel cell to power an entire home. Fuel cells, which generate electricity at about twice the efficiency of fossil-fuel-powered generation plants, have low emissions. In residential applications, they are expected to reduce the cost of electricity by 20 percent.

A fuel cell converts fuel (natural gas, gasoline, propane, ethanol, hydrogen, or other fuels) into direct current (DC) electrical energy. A conventional power plant produces electricity by burning fossil fuel to run a generator, which creates electricity. Fuel cells, on the other hand, bypass the combustion and generating processes and simply convert fuel into electricity, water, heat, carbon dioxide, and (depending on fuel type) a very small amount of nitrogen oxides, sulfur oxides, and particulate matter. With fuel cells, up to 80 percent of the energy obtained from fuel can be converted to usable electric power and heat (compared with about 40 percent from a central power plant). Waste heat from fuel cells can produce hot water or space heat for a home.

The target cost for residential fuel cells is $1,500 per kilowatt, although current prices are much higher. With the target initial cost, electricity from a 2-kilowatt system could provide all the power needed for a 3,000-square-foot home (with a good load management system) at 8 to 10 cents per kilowatt-hour over the lifetime of the fuel cell.

Residential fuel cells are not yet commercially available, although residential field trials are underway.

Chapter Five

Marketing
Energy- and Resource-Efficient Homes

Builders with green building practices should not underestimate the power of a good marketing campaign, because even the most energy-efficient home will not sell itself. Below are some techniques that have been successfully implemented by EVHA-winning builders. As industry marketing consultant Carrie Gehlbach, who also is former vice president of marketing for the 2000 EVHA Builder of the Year: San Antonio-based Medallion Homes, advises, "Marketing can't be something you do with leftover dollars. It has to be built into the budget on every single home, or it will end up getting cut."

Read on for ideas that can help you market energy efficiency. Try exploring a variety of marketing avenues, an approach that Gehlbach refers to as "cross-marketing."

Educating Customers and Sales Professionals

Because buyers may not be thinking about energy efficiency when they start looking for a home, it is helpful to show how living in an energy-efficient home will benefit them. Fortunately, capturing customers' attention may be easier than you think when energy efficiency is linked to cost savings. As Mike Beckett of Newmark Homes explains, "What's important to buyers is not just the mortgage payment, but the total cost of running a home. You can afford more

Figure 5.1 *A sales agent can easily explain construction details to customers with the aid of a model home with energy-efficient features shown in cutaways.*

home if your utility bill is lower." Beckett adds, "More home can mean living in a nicer community, buying a bigger house, or getting more amenities. Or you can simply have lower monthly total costs with an energy-efficient house."

Figure 5.2 *A model home includes educational information about energy efficient features.*

Many EVHA builders use spreadsheets to show consumers how the monthly mortgage plus utility costs can actually decrease with an energy-efficient home, even if mortgage costs rise slightly. Free software programs, such as ENERGY STAR's monthly cost calculation software, can help builders demonstrate monthly savings to home buyers. Other energy analysis software can help compare the estimated monthly energy costs of an efficient home with a conventional home.

A vital part of customer education is an informed sales staff and team of local sales professionals. A sales professional who believes in the benefits of resource- and energy-efficient construction may be one of the most effective marketing tools.

Walk-Throughs

Home tours can be an invaluable educational tool for both customers and sales professionals. Gabriel Enterprises of Newport News, Va., a 1999 EVHA winner, gives prospective home buyers a detailed walk-through of its homes during construction to help them understand the energy-efficient construction process. Other EVHA winners use their model homes to display detailed cutaways of energy features, such as wall sections. Wayne Homes of Uniontown, Ohio, a 2000 EVHA winner, uses cutaways of energy features such as insulation in its model homes. The cutaways show consumers the insulation thickness in Wayne Homes' projects versus competitors' homes. "Customers don't have to understand R-value and heat loss," explains Jeffrey Ury of Wayne Homes. "They can see the thickness of our insulation."

Training Sessions

Training workshops can be an effective tool for educating sales staff and real estate professionals. Slides, product samples, and energy bills are excellent aids that help sales professionals appreciate the energy-efficient features that are often invisible in a finished home. Be careful not to use technical terms without explaining them—if sales professionals do not understand how a feature works, they will not be able to explain it to prospective customers or, even worse, they may explain it incorrectly.

Publications

Another useful way to educate customers and sales professionals is by providing them with something they can take home. To show what their homes offer, some EVHA-winning builders give away copies of publications such as the annual EVHA magazine, reprints of the annual *Professional Builder* magazine article about

Figure 5.3 *A builder educates his sales staff on the jobsite about this home's energy-efficient features.*

the EVHA, checklists showing energy-efficient features, brochures, or books that detail construction practices and homeownership responsibilities for prospective buyers, sales staff, and local real estate professionals. Many builders also display copies of these publications in their model homes.

The Estridge Companies of Carmel, Ind., published a book titled *Construction Knowledge 101* that contains pictures, charts, and graphs intended to complement formal training sessions. The guide provides the reader with a fundamental understanding of the entire construction process—from legal considerations to the finishing touches—and is ideal for sales professionals and prospective customers. It is not limited to resource and energy efficiency but instead is a primer on the entire construction process.

Educating your customers and sales staff is an investment that requires extra time and up-front cost. However, Charlie Scott of the Estridge Companies feels that the effect of *Construction Knowledge 101* on the marketability of the firm's homes is well worth it. "When you care enough to educate people, it builds a whole new level of trust," Scott says. "Education helps build value into your homes—it helps customers know what to look for. It's hard to appreciate high performance if you don't know what performance is."

Advertising

EVHA-winning builders often explain energy efficiency in their advertising materials as a way to distinguish themselves from other builders. Advertising can teach customers about how an energy-efficient feature works and how it will benefit them. Advertisements for Salt Lake City, Utah's Watt Homes frequently feature a specific energy-efficient technology, such as raised-heel roof trusses or cellulose insulation. Watt's materials also often include a checklist of the home's energy-efficienct features, including what the competition is using (or not using).

Enid, Okla.-based Chisholm Creek Development's humorous postcard advertisements catch home buyers' attention and, at the same time, educate buyers about the benefits of energy efficiency. While the front of each postcard contains a catchy cartoon, the other side features educational information about energy efficiency. The marketing campaign is relatively inexpensive because the builder teamed up with the local utility company to develop the postcards.

The Estridge Companies of Indiana builds 500 homes a year and, in addition to being a 1996 EVHA winner, is a past winner of the National Housing Quality Award. The company publishes *Construction Knowledge 101*, a step-by-step guide to new home construction, for distribution to the firm's sales staff and potential customers. The book is so popular that Estridge receives requests for it every day.

If you've ever thought about offering a guide for your customers, it's not out of your reach. Although Scott says that it took hundreds of staff hours and between $10,000 and $20,000 to produce Construction Knowledge 101, there are other options available.

BuilderBooks at the NAHB works with companies in the home building industry to develop ideas and publish projects geared to help you better serve your partners and your customers, from business and construction tools and basics through customer service. For more information about publishing, call BuilderBooks at 800-368-5242.

Internet/CD Marketing

Because of the Internet and computers, many customers are becoming more educated about home building and buying. Gehlbach of Medallion Homes thinks that every builder should have a Web site. It does not have to be sophisticated or expensive, she says, just make it available. Gehlbach suggests enlisting the help of a high school student to develop the Web site.

Toasty House.
Or Living In
A Meat Locker.

Figure 5.4 *This postcard advertisement features a catchy cartoon and, on the back, contains information about energy*

Newmark Homes of Texas produces a CD-ROM containing a virtual home tour as well as information about energy-efficiency features and awards that the company has won. Although development costs can be significant, printing CDs is inexpensive. As a starting point, the CD can simply be a copy of a firm's Web site.

Free Publicity

Medallion Homes uses a wide variety of marketing approaches to get its message to buyers. But nothing is more cost effective, says Gehlbach, than free publicity. "Send a press release to your local media—newspapers, radio, and television. Local morning shows are always looking for stories, and they'll cover just about anything. We've had news coverage of a charity run that our company participated in and a

Figure 5.5 *Newmark Homes' CD-ROM details energy-efficient features of the firm's homes.*

school trip we hosted that taught kids about environmentally friendly construction. Of course, we sent the kids home with bags that included floor plans and price lists."

Energy Performance Guarantees

To convince customers that the cost savings are real, many EVHA winners offer utility cost guarantees. Guarantees can be a great way to sell customers on energy efficiency—even dubious clients pay attention to claims of energy cost savings that are backed by a guarantee.

EVHA builders have guaranteed energy costs through partnerships with outside companies such as:
- utilities;
- heating, ventilating, and air-conditioning (HVAC) contractors;
- product manufacturers;
- third-party consultants; and
- energy service companies that perform inspections, blower door tests, or duct leakage calculations.

Many of these partners can estimate a home's heating and cooling costs by evaluating the unit's design and conducting an inspection. They also may be able to back up a guarantee—lending credibility and ensuring payment if utility costs exceed prescribed thresholds. For example, through a relationship with Comfort Home Corporation, Gabriel Enterprises offers a one-year comfort warranty and a three-year guarantee on heating and cooling costs. Comfort Home pays any additional heating or cooling costs incurred above the guarantee.

> *Free publicity is everywhere. If you give the media a press release, it makes their job easier by providing them with a prepackaged story, and it makes your job easier by supplying free marketing.*
>
> *–Carrie Gehlbach,* consultant for Medallion Homes

Carl McIntyre of Carrington Homes in Greenfield, Ind., suggests working with a home energy rater when establishing energy cost guarantees. A home energy rater collects energy data from Carrington's projects and evaluates their performance. The rater may offer a guarantee, depending on the organization. When raters do not guarantee the costs, McIntyre looks to manufacturers; for example, Carrington's cellulose insulation manufacturer guarantees energy costs on homes built with its cellulose insulation.

Because other companies assume much of the risk involved in a guarantee, the offer of an energy cost guarantee can be easy and inexpensive for the builder. Carrington Homes pays only $300 more per home to allow the cellulose insulation contractor to handle everything, including testing and the guarantee itself. According to McIntyre, homeowners are generally receptive to

the extra cost. "[Cost guarantees] should always be done," he says. "To the homeowner, the small cost for testing is worth it—the resulting guarantee puts your money where your mouth is."

Figure 5.6 *Pulte Homes advertises its energy performance guarantees on a sign outside a model home.*

Financing and Energy Efficiency Mortgages

Given that energy efficiency often means higher up-front costs, prospective customers often think that they cannot afford an energy-efficient home. However, even if an energy-efficient home costs more, most home buyers can afford such a home because lower monthly utility costs often offset increased monthly mortgage payments. Many EVHA winners use financing as a marketing tool by advertising financial help, including energy efficiency mortgages (EEMs), for the purchase of resource- and energy-efficient homes.

Most EEMs give home buyers a higher ceiling ("stretch") in their debt-to-income ratio to account for the lower utility bills associated with energy-efficient features. With an EEM, homebuyers may be able to afford higher mortgage payments because they will save money on their utility bills each month. Watt Homes works with Western Colonial Mortgage, a local financial institution, to provide homebuyers with a 2 percent stretch through EEMs. Mitch Richardson of Watt Homes states that the firm also uses EEMs as a marketing tool. Watt advertisements explain how the stretch can increase customers' buying power, allowing more freedom and options in a new home.

Bill Siegel of Hampton Bay, N.Y.-based New Age Builders warns, however, that customers may be wary of the higher mortgage payments associated with EEMs. "People try to avoid the maximum [payment], and an EEM is going beyond the maximum. People aren't emotionally comfortable with that. Financially, it makes sense for the person to pay the extra up-front. That's how buyers are—if they can get a smaller mortgage, they will." He advises builders to make sure that buyers understand the value of an energy-efficient home and that the features are worth the added up-front cost.

E Seal, a national marketing alliance that was created by the Edison Electric Institute in Washington, D.C., and includes utilities and marketing partners, addresses some of Siegel's concerns. The E Seal Mortgage, available through participating E Seal utilities and energy-service providers, offers 100 percent financing of energy-efficient upgrades. Homeowners can thus buy a home with energy-efficient upgrades without increasing the down payment or private mortgage insurance requirement. Other benefits of the E Seal Mortgage include lower closing costs and lower interest rates.

E Seal Mortgages also give builders an incentive to add energy-efficiency features. Tom Farkas of EEI states that with an E Seal Mortgage, "It's in the builder's best interest to add as many energy-efficient features as possible, as long as the upgrades are cost effective."

Understandably many builders fear that the increased

> *The first step in starting to build energy-efficient homes is to find a partner. Join* ENERGY STAR, *a utility program, a manufacturer program, a home builder's association, or an energy conservation group. Across the board, the best builders of energy-efficient homes partnered with other folks and the reason is two-fold. First, these programs provide technical support and ideas; second, making a commitment to another organization makes you committed as well.*
>
> — **Charlie Scott,** *Estridge Companies*

costs of energy efficiency features will drive customers away. The E Seal Mortgage provides an opportunity for builders to offer energy-efficiency features separately from other amenities. As Farkas puts it, "You don't have to trade off energy efficiency for a hot tub."

Partnerships for Energy Efficiency

Partnerships can ease the transition to energy-efficient home construction by providing technical support and cementing the commitment to build energy-efficient homes. Past EVHA winners have had success in teaming with several energy programs described below.

Figure 5.7 *An ENERGY STAR logo is proudly attached to every home built by Stitt Energy Systems.*

ENERGY STAR labeled homes, which is a collaboration among the U.S. Environmental Protection Agency (EPA), the U.S. Department of Energy (DOE), and the private sector, is designed to help consumers find and purchase energy-efficient homes. Participating home builders benefit from the program's prepackaged marketing tools and home energy ratings that help differentiate ENERGY STAR builders from their competitors. According to Sam Rashkin, EPA program manager, "ENERGY STAR is a simple and effective way for builders to communicate the value of energy efficiency to home buyers."

Gabriel Enterprises, a Virginia builder of affordable homes, is an ENERGY STAR builder and strong advocate of energy-efficient home construction. Jay Epstein, president, uses the ENERGY STAR labeled homes in his marketing efforts. The builder attributes much of his company's strong growth to its niche in the energy-efficient market and participation with ENERGY STAR. The company has grown from building 16 houses annually in the early 1990s to about 120 houses in 1999. "The locomotive is rolling and will be hard to stop," says Epstein.

> **R**ogers, Arkansas-based Stitt Energy Systems proudly displays the ENERGY STAR logo on jobsite signs, in its office, and on its letterhead. Every Stitt Energy Systems home is outfitted with an antique-bronze ENERGY STAR placard.

Many EVHA-winning builders sign up as ENERGY STAR partners to help market their homes because the use of the widely recognized ENERGY STAR logo provides brand recognition. According to Rashkin, "Because of brand name labeling, ENERGY STAR gives builders a way to differentiate their homes to consumers who wouldn't otherwise consider energy efficiency." The rating that each home receives as part of the program is much like the miles per gallon rating given to new automobiles, thus giving the home buyer an easy tool to evaluate a home's energy efficiency. For more information about the ENERGY STAR labeled homes and how to participate, visit www.energystar.gov or call 888-STAR-YES.

> *Partnerships have been of great value to us, not only in developing the appropriate energy-saving construction techniques, but also in lending credence, support, and enhancement of our consumer-oriented messages.*
>
> *– Dave Beck, Pulte Home Corp.*

Pruett Builders of Sarasota, Fla., built a home to the American Lung Association's (ALA) Health House standards and won a 2000 EVHA award. The winning home contained features designed to:

- minimize particulate matter and biological contaminants;
- control indoor humidity and air infiltration;
- reduce volatile organic compound (VOC) emissions; and
- increase energy and resource efficiency.

According to Brian Pruett, president of Pruett Builders, the ALA program increased the marketability of the company's home through local publicity, consumer marketing materials provided by the program and by offering consumers an option that was not available elsewhere. Builders can find out more about the Health House program, by visiting www.healthhouse.org or calling the American Lung Association of Minnesota at 651-227-8014.

Figure 5.8 *ENVIRONMENTS FOR LIVING program.*

Several past EVHA-winning home builders participate in Building America––a partnership between the U.S. DOE and builders that encourages energy- and resource-efficient construction. Large volume builders, such as Pulte Home Corporation-Las Vegas division, recognized the potential competitive advantages associated with Building America and seized the opportunity to join the partnership.

According to Dave Beck, director of construction for the Pulte Home Corp.-Las Vegas division, "Partnerships have been of great value to us, not only in developing the appropriate energy-saving construction techniques, but also in lending credence, support, and enhancement of our consumer-oriented messages." To find out more about Building America, visit www.eren.doe.gov/buildings/Building_America.

Treating a home as a system rather than as a collection of individual components is the central theme behind GreenStone Industries' ENVIRONMENTS FOR LIVING program. The program certifies homes in three categories (silver, gold, and platinum) depending on level of insulation, ventilation, and air tightness. The program provides marketing support in the form of Web site listings, promotional materials, sample press releases, and customized promotional support. In addition, an energy cost guarantee is applied to qualifying homes. The 2000 EVHA Builder of the Year, Medallion Homes, joined the ENVIRON-

Figure 5.9 *Blower door tests are required for most home energy ratings and usually cost $200 or more.*

MENTS FOR LIVING program after earning a 1999 EVHA Honorable Mention award. Seeking a gold award, Medallion reevaluated its practices. The company credits ENVIRONMENTS FOR LIVING for dramatically improving its winning home's performance. Gehlbach says the guarantee "is one of the biggest things" the firm has done in its marketing efforts in the recent past.

Builders wishing to join the program should expect to pay at least $200 for plan reviews. Verification testing costs about $175 to $250 per test. For more information about participating in the ENVIRONMENTS FOR LIVING program, contact GreenStone at 888-592-7684 or www.greenstone.com.

Demonstrating Energy Efficiency through Diagnostic Testing

Just how energy efficient is a home? Until a home is occupied, it is tough to answer that question. Fortunately, several tools are available to help demonstrate how efficiency works and, more importantly, how it affects a customer's bottom line. Blower door testing, duct leakage testing, and infrared thermography are useful tools for determining the need for air sealing as well as compliance with design or program standards (such as a utility's home-efficiency program), and for diagnosing comfort, indoor air quality, and durability problems.

Figure 5.10 *Duct leakage testing is less common than blower door testing but can also be used to demonstrate a home's energy efficiency. Tests can be performed on new houses before drywall installation at a cost of about $175 to $400.*

However, the average homeowner usually does not understand the results of the tests. Yet, some builders find that conducting tests in the presence of prospective home buyers helps customers understand the meaning of test results. "It is an excellent marketing tool," says Perry DeSiato, vice president of land acquisition for Newton, Pa.-based DeLuca Enterprises. "It is a great 'dog and pony show' for the homeowner; they get to see energy efficiency for themselves."

Figure 5.11 *Infrared thermography is another handy diagnostic tool that detects a home's relative heat loss and air leakage. Warm objects appear brighter on the high-contrast infrared images, showing consumers where heat escapes from a home. The cost for infrared testing is about $200 to $500.*

While typical customers might not understand what the test results mean, they can understand more about energy efficiency and diagnostic testing when they see tests performed and view the results in com parison with typical construction in their area. To find out more about these tests, check with your local utility company (it may offer free or discounted services), building consultants, or manufacturers of testing equipment.

Conclusion

There are many things conventional builders can do to design, build, and market more energy- and resource-efficient homes. The examples in this guide are intended to lend ideas and inspiration for building more energy and resource efficiently. The first step is to be interested and to start learning. The next step is to learn more and to start doing. Use the resources contained in this guide and develop your own ideas.

Whatever you do, be sure to get recognized for your efforts by applying for the National Green Building Awards. For more information about the award program or to request an application, contact the NAHB Research Center at 800-638-8556, by e-mail at ngba@nahbrc.org, or visit www.nahbrc.org.

EnergyValue Housing Award Notables

EnergyValue Housing Award Partners

National Association of Home Builders
1201 15th Street, NW
Washington, DC 20005-2800
www.nahb.com

National Renewable Energy Laboratory (NREL)
1617 Cole Boulevard
Golden, CO 80401
(303) 384-6191
www.nrel.gov

NAHB Research Center
400 Prince George's Blvd.
Upper Marlboro, MD 20774
(301) 249-4000
www.nahbrc.org

U.S. Department of Energy
1000 Independence Avenue, SW
Washington, DC 20585
www.doe.gov

Professional Builder
1350 East Touhy Avenue
Des Plaines, IL 60018
(847) 390-2105
www.probuilder.com

EnergyValue Housing Award 2002 Sponsors

Broan-NuTone LLC
926 W. State Street
PO Box 140
Hartford, WI 53027
(262) 673-4340
www.broan.com

GreenFiber
809 W Hill St Ste A
Charlotte, NC 28208
(704) 379-0653 12
www.greenstone.com

Icyene, Inc.
5805 Whittle Road
Suite 110
Mississauga, Ontario, L4Z 2J1
(905) 890-7325, ext. 204
www.icynene.com

JM Huber-Engineered Woods Division
10925 David Taylor Drive
Suite 300
Charlotte, NC 28262
(800) 933-9220
www.huber.com

TechShield by LP
10115 Kincey Avenue
Suite 150
Huntersville, NC 28078
(704) 948-1451
www.techshield.lpcorp.com

United Technologies-Carrier Corporation
7310 West Morris Street
Indianapolis, IN 46206-0070
(317) 240-5277
www.carrier.com

EnergyValue Housing Award Winners

Able Development Corp. DBA
Able Homebuilders
4408 Lost Meadows Road
Sioux City, IA 51108-1000
(712) 281-4663

AF Sterling
3573 East Sunrise, Suite 209
Tucson, AZ 85718
(520) 577-6605

Amhome USA, Inc.
22646 Weeks Boulevard
P.O. Box 1492
Land O' Lakes, FL 34639
(813) 996-4660
www.amhomeusa.com

Arkin Homes, Inc.
100 East Street, Southeast
Vienna, VA 22180-4800
(703) 848-2735

Artistic Homes
4420 Tower Road SW
Albuquerque, NM 87121
(505) 247-8400

**Barco Realty and
Development Company**
8 Old County Road
Plymouth, MA 02360
(508) 888-2274

BBH Enterprises, Inc.
2718 Wagonwheel Drive
Carrollton, TX 75006
(972) 418-7772
www.envirocustomhomes.com

**Best Homes
Division of Davis Homes LLC**
3755 East 82nd Street
Suite 120
Indianapolis, IN 46240

(317) 595-2909
www.besthomesindy.com

Bigelow Group, Inc.
999 South Plum Grove Road
Palatine, IL 60067
(847) 705-6400
www.bigelowhomes.com

**Bill Eich Construction
Company**
1706 Lincoln Avenue
P.O. Box S
Spirit Lake, IA 51360
(712) 336-4438

Bob Buckner Homes
P.O. Box 582
Mustang, OK 73064
(405) 376-2050

Bruce Davis, Inc.
2701 Cambridge Court
P.O. Box 1008
La Plata, MD 20646
(301) 870-2400

Carrington Homes, Inc.
3617 West US Highway 40
Greenfield, IN 46140-9591
(317) 467-0008

Casa Verde Custom Homes
9600 Wilshire Avenue, Northeast
Albuquerque, NM 87122
(505) 242-0606
www.casaverdehomes.com

**Chisholm Creek
Development, LLC**
502 Chisholm Creek
P.O. Box 1586
Enid, OK 73701
(580) 242-3400

75

Christian Builders, Inc.
21000 Rogers Drive
Rogers, MN 55374
(612) 428-8323

Colorado Dream Homes, LLC
2283 West Highway 160
P.O. Box 2997
Pagosa Springs, CO 81147
(970) 731-3071
www.coloradodreamhomesllc.com

Columbia Builders, Inc.
P.O. Box 999
Columbia, MD 21044
(410) 730-3939

Decker Homes
2666 Sterns Road
P.O. Box 98
Lambertville, MI 48144
(313) 856-2663

DeLuca Enterprises
842 Durham Road, Suite 200
Newtown, PA 18940-9682
(215) 598-3451

Dewees Builders, Inc.
46 41st Avenue
Isle of Palms, SC 29451
(843) 886-4365
www.deweesisland.com

**Distinctive Homes of
Southwest Florida**
4395 Corporate Square
Naples, FL 33942
(941) 643-5739

Dominion Building Group, Inc.
145 Burford Avenue
P.O. Box 360
Virginia Beach, VA 23458-0360
(757) 491-5592

DPO Construction
4268 Turkey Creek Road
Iowa City, IA 52240
(319) 351-2879

Emerald Homes
333 Sam Houston Parkway East,
Suite 1405
Houston, TX 77060
(713) 999-2977

ERA Bob Ward Realty
2700 Philadelphia Road
Edgewood, MD 21040-1120
(410) 679-5000

Estridge Companies
1041 West Main Street
Carmel, IN 46032
(317) 582-2431
www.estridge.com

**Fallman Design and
Construction**
11137 Versailles Boulevard
Clermont, FL 34711
(352) 394-5555

Fleetwood Homes of Oregon
2655 Progress Way
PO Box 628
Woodburn, OR 97071
(503) 981-3136

Gabriel Enterprises, Inc.
3606 Acorn Avenue, Suite 200
Newport News, VA 23185
(757) 245-7351

Gimme Shelter Construction
1599 County ZZ
P.O. Box 176
Amherst Junction, WI 54407
(715) 677-4289

GreenVillage Company
129 Mount Auburn Street
Cambridge, MA 02138
(617) 491-1888

Hall Quality Homes
P.O. Box 1987
Palmer, AK 99645
(907) 746-2757
www.hallqualityhomes.com

Hidden Springs Building Company
5892 W. Hidden Springs Drive
Hidden Springs, ID 83703
(208) 229-2323

HKW Enterprises
4707 Northwest 53rd Avenue
Suite A
Gainesville, FL 32606
www.hkwbuilders.com

Holdridge Homes
578 Harrison
Perrysburg, OH 43551
(419) 874-8803
www.holdridgehomes.com

Holloway Company
1022 Ridgeway Drive
Wichita Falls, TX 76306-6941
(940) 592-3107

Ideal Homes of Norman, LLC
1320 North Porter
Norman, OK 73071
(405) 364-1152
www.ideal-homes.com

Image Homes Corporation
P.O. Box 1028
Evergreen, CO 80437-1028
(303) 670-1906

Kendall Homes, Inc.
1518 Thistle Lane
Fort Wayne, IN 46825
(219) 486-4429

Koehnemann Construction, Inc.
439 Grace Avenue
Panama City, FL 32401
(850) 769-3419

The Lee Group and Braemar Urban Ventures
310 Washington Boulevard,
Suite D214
Marina Del Rey, CA 90292
(310) 827-0171

Mavor Design and Construction, Inc.
7007 Bristol Lane
Bozeman, MT 59715
(406) 585-3711

McGurn Investment Company
101 Southeast 2nd Place
Suite 202
Gainesville, FL 32601
(352) 372-6172

McNaughton Homes
4400 Deer Path Road, Suite 201
Harrisburg, PA 17110
(717) 234-4000

Medallion Homes
6929 Camp Bullis Road
San Antonio, TX 78256
(210) 494-2555
www.medallionhomes.com

Melvin and Sons Contractors
1516 Tennessee Avenue
Lynn Haven, FL 32444
(850) 265-2328

Neal Carter and Sun, Inc.
(207) 285-3138

New Age Builders, Inc.
186 West Montauk Highway,
Suite D11
Hampton Bay, NY 11946
(516) 728-6644

New Haven Construction
1485 Commerce Park Drive,
Suite B
Tipp City, OH 45371
(937) 667-1621

Newmark Homes
1200 Soldiers Field Drive
Sugar Land, TX 77479
(281) 243-0100
www.newmarkhomes.com

NVR (Ryan Homes)
210 Carroll Street
Thurmont, MD 21788
(301) 271-3189

Pons Construction
322 Hidden Island Drive
Panama City Beach, FL 32408
(850) 230-6611
www.ponsconstruction.com

Pringle Development
26600 Ace Avenue
Leesburg, FL 34748
(352) 365-2303

Pruett Builders, Inc.
3801 Bee Ridge Road, Suite 8
Sarasota, FL 34233
(941) 922-4700

**Pulte Home Corporation-
Las Vegas Division**
1635 Village Center Circle,
Suite 250
Las Vegas, NV 89134
(702) 256-7900

Pulte Home Corporation-
PC/BRE Springfield LLC
6495 South St. Andrews Blvd.
Chandler, AZ 85249
(480) 802-6999

**Pulte Home Corporation -
Phoenix Division**
10235 S. 51st Street, Suite 100
Phoenix, AZ 85044
(480) 598-2100

**Pulte Home Corporation-
Tucson Division**
7493 North Oracle Road
Suite 115
Tucson, AZ 85704
(520) 797-1100

RE Collier-Builder
9415 Hull Street Road, Suite E
Richmond, VA 23236
(804) 276-4134

**Redman/Moduline Homes-A
Champion Company**
2701 Cambridge Court
Suite 220
Auburn Hills, MI 48326
(248) 276-1459

RJT Builders
1425 East University Drive
Phoenix, AZ 85034
(602) 257-1656

Ron Putman Construction, Inc.
P.O. Box 28375
Panama City, FL 32411
(850) 234-3930

Russell Home Builders
437 Twin Bay Drive
Pensacola, FL 32534
(850) 477-9789

Schultz Construction
8900 South 56th Street
Lincoln, NE 68516
(402) 430-6020

Shaw Homes, Inc.
233 South Wacker Drive,
Suite 325
Chicago, IL 60606
(312) 382-8800

Solarco
8301 Six Forks Road
Raleigh, NC 27615
(919) 847-6998

South Wall Builders
P.O. Box 100
Missoula, MT 59806
(406) 721-5926

State of the Art Builders
1035 Butternut Lane
Oneida, WI 54155-9120
(920) 662-0826

Stitt Energy Systems
1301 South 8th Street
Rogers, AR 72756-5331
(501) 636-8745
www.stittenergy.com

Stoltzfus Enterprises, Ltd
985 North Penn Drive
West Chester, PA 19380
(610) 692-3888

Thayer Street Associates, Inc.
10 Thayer St
P.O. Box 146
South Deerfield, MA 01373
(413) 665-4018

Tierra Concrete Homes, Inc.
P.O. Box 1924
Pueblo, CO 81002-1924
(719) 947-3040
www.tierraconcretehomes.com

Timbers to Trim Carpentry
304 Longhill Road
West Brookfield, MA 01585
(413) 436-5104

U.S. Home Colorado Division
6000 Greenwood Plaza Boulevard
Englewood, CO 80111-4816
(303) 779-6100

US Home Corporation
5151 East Broadway, Suite 100
Tucson, AZ 85711
(520) 747-0997

Valley Manufactured Housing
1717 South Fourth Street
Sunnyside, WA 98944
(509) 839-9409
www.valleymanufacturedhousing.com

**Watt Homes a Division
of WL Homes**
3653 West 1987 South,
Building 7
Salt Lake City, UT 84104
(801) 288-1844
www.watthomes.com

Wayne Homes, LLC
3777 Boettler Oaks Drive
Uniontown, OH 44685
(330) 896-7611
www.waynehomes.com

West Slope Panel Homes, LLC
190 Cattle Drive
Victor, MT 59875
(406) 642-6669

Yorktown 1781 Developers
4000 Naamans Creek Road
Boothwyn, PA 19061

Green Building Resources

Organizations

**American Council for an
Energy-Efficient Economy**
1001 Connecticut Avenue, NW,
Suite 801
Washington, DC 20036
(202) 429-0063
www.aceee.org

**American Society of Heating,
Refrigeration, and
Air-Conditioning Engineers**
1791 Tullie Circle, NE
Atlanta, GA 30329
(800) 527-4723
www.ashrae.org

American Solar Energy Society
2400 Central Avenue, Suite G-1
Boulder, CO 80301
(303) 443-3130
www.ases.org

**Building America Program
U.S. Department of Energy**
Office of Building Systems, EE-41
1000 Independence Avenue, SW
Washington, DC 20585-0121
(202) 586-9472
*www.eren.doe.gov/buildings/
Building_America*

**Cellulose Insulation
Manufacturers Association**
133 South Keowee Street
Dayton, OH 45402
(937) 222-2462
www.cellulose.org

**Center for Renewable Energy
and Sustainable Technology**
www.solstice.crest.org

**Energy Efficiency and Renewable
Energy Clearinghouse**
P.O. Box 3048
Merrifield, VA 22116
(800) 363-3732 (DOE-EREC)

**Energy Efficiency and Renewable
Energy Network**
U.S. Department of Energy
www.eren.doe.gov

**Energy Efficient Building
Association**
490 Concordia Avenue
St. Paul, MN 55103-2441
(651) 268-7585
www.eeba.org

Energy Rated Homes of America
(907) 345-1930
www.resnet.org

ENERGY STAR labeled homes
(888) STAR-YES
www.epa.gov/energystar.html

Fuel Cells 2000
1625 K Street, NW, Suite 790
Washington, DC 20006
(202) 785-9620
www.fuelcells.org

Geothermal Heat Pump Consortium
701 Pennsylvania Avenue, NW
Washington, DC 20004
(202) 508-5500
www.geoexchange.org

Hydronics Institute
35 Russo Place
P.O. Box 218
Berkley Heights, NJ 07922
(908) 464-8200
www.gamanet.org

Insulating Concrete Forms Association
1807 Glenview Road, Suite 203
Glenview, IL 60025
(847) 657-9730
www.forms.org

NAHB Research Center, Inc.
EnergyValue Housing Award
(800) 638-8556
www.nahbrc.org
evha@nahbrc.org

NAHB Research Center, Inc.
ToolBase Services
(800) 898-2842
www.nahbrc.org

National Insulation Association
99 Canal Center Plaza, Suite 222
Alexandria, VA 22314
(703) 683-6422
www.insulation.org

National Renewable Energy Laboratory
Center for Buildings and
Thermal Systems
1617 Cole Boulevard
Golden, CO 80401
(303) 275-3000
www.nrel.gov

North Carolina Solar Center
Box 7401
North Carolina State University
Raleigh, NC 27695-7401
(919) 515-3480
www.ncsc.ncsu.edu

Portland Cement Association
5420 Old Orchard Road
Skokie, IL 60077
(888) 333-4840
www.concretehomes.org

Solar Energy Industries Association
122 C Street, NW, 4th Floor
Washington, DC 20001-2109
(202) 383-2600
www.seia.org

Structural Insulated Panel Association
(253) 858-7472
www.sips.org

Sustainable Building Industries Council
1331 H Street, NW, Suite 1000
Washington, DC 20005
(202) 628-7400
www.sbicouncil.org

Books

Manual D: Residential Duct Systems. Air Conditioning Contractors Association, Washington, DC.

Manual J: Residential Load Calculation. Air Conditioning Contractors Association, Washington, DC.

Manual S: Residential Equipment Selection. Air Conditioning Contractors Association, Washington, DC.

Manual T: Air distribution basics for Residential and Small Commercial Buildings. Air Conditioning Contractors Association, Washington, DC.

A Builder's Guide to Placement of Ducts and HVAC Equipment in Conditioned Space. (2000). Upper Marlboro, MD: NAHB Research Center, Inc.

A Builder's Guide to Marketable Affordable Durable Entry-Level Homes to Last. (1998). Upper Marlboro, MD: NAHB Research Center, Inc.

A Builder's Guide to Residential HVAC Systems. (1997). Upper Marlboro, MD: NAHB Research Center, Inc.

Bower, John. (1997). *The Healthy House.* Bloomington, IN: The Healthy House Institute.

Bower, John. (1995). *Understanding Ventilation: How to Design, Select, and Install Residential Ventilation Systems.* Bloomington, IN: The Healthy House Institute.

Brookbank, George. (1992). *Desert Landscaping: How to Start and Maintain a Healthy Landscape in the Southwest.* Tucson: University of Arizona Press.

Builders Guide to Home Lighting, (1995). Lighting Research Center Rensselaer Polytechnic Institute, Troy, NY.

Cost Effective Home Building A Design and Construction Handbook (1994). Upper Marlboro, MD: NAHB Research Center, Inc.

Carmody, John; Stephen Selkowitz; and Lisa Heschong. (1996). *Residential Windows: A Guide to New Technologies and Energy Performance.* New York: W.W. Norton and Co.

Crosbie, Michael J., ed. (1997). *The Passive Solar Design and Construction Handbook.* New York: John Wiley.

Design Guide for Frost Protected Shallow Foundations. (1996). Upper Marlboro, MD: NAHB Research Center, Inc.

Guide to Developing Green Building Programs. (1999). Upper Marlboro, MD: NAHB Research Center, Inc.

Harwood, Barbara Bannon. (1997). *The Healing House.* Carlsbad, CA: Hay House.

Leslie, Russell P. and Kathryn Conway. (1996). *The Lighting Pattern Book for Homes.* Lighting Research Center Rensselaer Polytechnic Institute. Troy, NY.

Lstiburek, Joe; and Betsy Pettit. (1999). *EEBA Builder's Guide—Cold Climate.* Minneapolis: Energy Efficient Building Association.

Lstiburek, Joe; and Betsy Pettit. (1999). *EEBA Builder's Guide—Mixed-Humid Climates.* Minneapolis: Energy Efficient Building Association.

Lstiburek, Joe; and Betsy Pettit. (1999). *EEBA Builder's Guide—Hot-Arid Climate.* Minneapolis: Energy Efficient Building Association.

Moffat, Anne Simon, et al. (1994). *Energy Efficient and Environmental Landscaping.* Appropriate Solution Press.

Passive Solar Industries Council, National Renewable Energy Laboratory, and Charles Eley Associates. (1994). *Passive Solar Design Strategies: Guidelines for Home Building.* Washington, DC: Passive Solar Industries Council.

Residential Construction Waste Management: A Builder's Field Guide. (1999). Upper Marlboro, MD: NAHB Research Center, Inc.

Roth, Sally. (1997). *Natural Landscaping.* Emmaus, PA: Rodale Press.

Selected Construction Regulations for the Home Building Industry. Washington, DC: U.S. Department of Labor, Occupational Safety and Health Administration.

Sustainable Building Sourcebook. Austin, TX: City of Austin Green Builder Program. www.greenbuilder.com/sourcebook.

Waite, Timothy, J. (1994). *Cost Effective Home Building: A Design and Construction Handbook.* Washington, DC: Home Builder Press.

Warde, John. (1997). *The Healthy House Handbook.* Random House.

Wilson, Alex; and John Morrill. (Annual). *Consumer Guide to Home Energy Savings.* Washington, DC: American Council for an Energy-Efficient Economy.

Magazines, Journals, and Newsletters

Automated Builder
1445 Donlon, Suite 16
Ventura, CA 93003
(805) 642-9735
www.modularcenter.com/abmag

Energy Design Update
(800) 964-5118
www.cutter.com/edu

EnergyValue Housing Award
NAHB Research Center, Inc.
400 Prince George's Boulevard
Upper Marlboro, MD 20774
(800) 638-8556
E-mail: *evha@nahbrc.org*
www.nahbrc.org

Environmental Building News
Environmental Building News
122 Birge Street, Suite 30
Brattleboro, VT 05301
(80) 257-7300
E-mail: info@buildinggreen.com
www.buildinggreen.com

*Environmental Design and
Construction*
P.O. Box 3304
Northbrook, IL 60065-3304
www.edcmag.com

Fine Homebuilding
The Taunton Press, Inc.
63 South Main Street
P.O. Box 5506
Newtown, CT 06470
(203) 426-8171 or
(800) 243-7252

Home Energy Magazine
2124 Kittredge Street, Suite 95
Berkeley, CA 94704
(510) 524-5405
www.homeenergy.org

Home Power
P.O. Box 520
Ashland, OR 97520
www.homepower.com

Journal of Light Construction
RR #2
Box 146
Richmond, VT 05477
(800) 552-1951
www.jlconline.com

Nation's Building News
National Association of
Home Builders
1201 15th Street, NW
Washington, DC 20005-2841
(800) 368-5242
www.nahb.com

Popular Science
(800) 289-9399
www.popularscience.com

Professional Builder
Cahners Publishing
1350 East Touhy Avenue
Des Plaines, IL 60018
www.probuilder.com

Solar Today
Journal of the American
Solar Energy Society
2400 Central Avenue
G-1 Boulder, CO 80301
(303) 443-3130
www.ases.org

ToolBase News
NAHB Research Center, Inc.
400 Prince George's Boulevard
Upper Marlboro, MD 20774
(800) 898-2842
www.toolbase.org

<u>Appendix C</u>

Glossary

Active solar energy system: A system that harnesses energy from the sun by using an additional source of energy, such as electricity, to operate fans and pumps.

Advanced framing: A method of framing that minimizes the use of wood resources and improves insulation at corners and window and door headers. Also called Optimum Value Engineering.

Air barrier: A material or structural element that inhibits airflow into and out of a building's envelope but allows water vapor to pass through. To create an air barrier, a continuous sheet of polyethylene, extruded polystyrene, or polypropylene is wrapped around the outside of a house during construction.

Air changes per hour (ACH): Measure of the air leakage rate of a building, specifically the number of times each hour that the total volume of air in a building is replaced with outdoor air. Technicians usually measure ACH by pressurizing or depressurizing the house to 50 Pascals. Often expressed as ACH_{50} (air changes per hour at 50 Pascals pressure).

Air leakage: The uncontrolled flow of air into or out of a building through gaps in the building structure.

Air sealing: The prevention of unintentional airflow into or out of a building through the use of foam, gaskets, caulk, tape, or other materials. Typical locations for air sealing include areas around doors and windows, under sill plates, around rim joists, and at utility penetrations.

Airtight drywall approach: A building construction technique that creates a continuous air retarder by using drywall, gaskets, and caulking. Gaskets are used in place of caulking to seal drywall to top and bottom plates.

Annual fuel utilization efficiency (AFUE): The measure of seasonal or annual efficiency of a residential heating furnace or boiler that takes into account the cyclic on/off operation. The higher the number, the more efficient is the heating equipment.

Backdrafting: The flow of air down a flue or chimney and into a house when combustion appliances lack make-up air (usually because of simultaneous operation of exaust fans and fireplaces or combustion appliances). Very tight buildings are more susceptible to backdrafting if combustion equipment is not properly vented.

Blower door: A large fan placed in an exterior doorway for use by energy auditors to pressurize (or depressurize) a building for the purpose of locating places of air leakage and energy loss. Air leakage is usually expressed in air changes per hour, cubic feet per minute, or effective leakage area.

Building envelope: The structural elements (walls, roof, floor, foundation) of a building that enclose conditioned space; the building shell.

California corner: An advanced framing technique that uses two studs (instead of the usual three) to make an exterior corner. The technique requires fewer resources and results in more insulation at corners while saving the builder money.

Capacity: The amount of energy demand (usually heating or cooling) that equipment can meet or supply.

Coefficient of performance (COP): A measure of the efficiency of a heat pump or air conditioner expressed as the amount of energy output per unit of energy input. The higher the COP, the more efficient is the device.

Combination system: A heating system that uses the domestic water heater for both water and space heating. Hot water is typically piped to a heat exchanger (coil), where a fan blows air over the coil to produce heated air.

Condensing furnaces or boilers: High-efficiency heating systems that extract a high percentage of the available energy from gas combustion by recovering heat from combustion products. Water vapor in the combustion products condenses to liquid water before leaving the furnace and must be drained.

Conditioned space: Area within a house that is heated or cooled. Conditioned space is separated from unconditioned space by a thermal envelope.

Conduction: The transfer of heat through a solid material.

Convection: The transfer of heat by means of air currents or other fluid motion.

Degree day: The difference between the outdoor daily average temperature from an assumed base temperature, normally taken as 65 degrees Fahrenheit.

Desuperheater: A device that takes waste heat from the condenser of a heat pump or air conditioner and uses it for heating domestic water.

Direct vent heater: A type of combustion heating system that draws combustion air directly from outside and vents the products of combustion directly outside. These systems are beneficial in tight, energy-efficient homes because they do not depressurize a home and do not cause air infiltration or backdrafting of other combustion appliances.

Duct leakage testing equipment: Diagnostic equipment that pressurizes a duct system and measures the extent of air leakage.

E Seal: The electric utility industry's energy efficiency and environmental housing initiative. The core of the program is its certification system, which ensures that electric utilities' new construction programs exceed the highest nationally recognized energy efficiency and environmental criteria.

Energy efficiency mortgage (EEM): A type of home mortgage that takes into account lower monthly utility bills as a result of energy-efficiency improvements. Because of projected reductions in monthly utility bills, a borrower can qualify for a larger loan than would otherwise be possible.

Energy efficiency ratio (EER): Instantaneous, steady-state efficiency of air conditioners measured under standard test conditions. EER is the amount of cooling provided per unit of electricity purchased. The higher the EER, the more efficient is the air conditioner.

Energy factor (EF): Overall efficiency of a water heater or other appliance. EF is defined differently for different appliances; however, the higher the energy factor number, the more efficient is water heater.

Energy recovery ventilator: A mechanical ventilation system that provides controlled ventilation to a building. It includes an integral heat exchanger that recovers heat (both sensible and latent) from the outgoing air.

Energy Star home: A home that is predicted to use 30 percent less energy than houses built to the Model Energy Code (MEC) while maintaining or improving indoor air quality. The Energy Star Home Program is an Environmental Protection Agency and Department of Energy program.

Energy truss: See *raised-heel roof truss.*

Engineered wood: Any of several manufactured products that use wood and binders to create high-strength direct substitutes for wood. "Engineered" refers to the manufacturing process, not to the use of the product. Engineered wood creates less waste at the mill than solid-sawn lumber and reduces job site waste.

Flex-duct: Flexible ductwork made with an inner liner, a layer of insulation, and an outer covering of plastic.

Frost-protected shallow foundation (FPSF): A foundation system in which foam insulation is placed around the perimeter of a foundation to reduce heat loss through the slab and/or below-grade walls, thereby raising the frost depth of a building and allowing foundations to be as shallow as 16 inches below grade.

Gasket: Rubber or foam material that is placed to inhibit airflow through areas that are typically leaky, such as electrical outlets located on exterior walls and under sill plates.

Geothermal system: A heat pump that uses the ground or water as a heat source or sink. Efficiency is improved over air-source heat pumps because the temperature of the ground or water is more constant and moderate than that of the air. Geothermal systems typically incorporate some method to contribute heat to the domestic hot water system.

Heat pump: Similar to an air conditioner but capable of operating in reverse to heat as well as cool. A heat pump transfers heat (usually from the air) from one location to another.

Heat recovery or energy recovery ventilator (HRV/ERV): Engineered venting system that recovers useful energy from exhaust air.

Heating degree days (HDD): The number of degrees per day that the daily average temperature falls below a base temperature, usually 65 degrees Fahrenheit. Total HDD is the cumulative total for the year or heating season.

Heating seasonal performance factor (HSPF): Efficiency of a heat pump in the heating mode, taking cycling into account. HSPF is the amount of heating (Btu) provided per unit of electricity purchased (kWh). The higher the HSPF number, the more efficient is the heat pump.

High-efficiency particle accumulator: An air filter that captures a high percentage of all particles, including extremely small particles not captured by other types of filters.

Home energy rating system: A collection of programs throughout the country that assign energy ratings based on a home's predicted energy use. Ratings are usually on a scale of either one to 100 points or one to five-plus stars. Most houses built today without any special attention to energy efficiency typically earn an 80-point or three-star rating.

Housewrap: See *air barrier.*

Infrared thermography: A technique capable of detecting infrared wavelengths. Infrared thermography is used to detect temperature variations on a surface and to identify areas of heat loss from a building.

Insulating concrete form (ICF): Concrete form-wall constructed of foam insulation that remains in place after the concrete cures.

Latent cooling load: The load created by moisture in the air, including moisture from outside air infiltration and indoor sources such as occupants, plants, cooking, or showering.

Latent heat: Heat released or absorbed by a process that does not involve a temperature change, such as condensation.

Load: The energy consumption or requirement of a piece or group of equipment.

Low-emittance (Low-E) coatings: A coating applied to the surface of the glazing of a window to reduce the heat transfer through the window. A low-E coating is applied to various surfaces of a window depending on the climate and desired effect.

Manual D: ACCA manual for designing residential duct systems.

Manual J: Method developed by ACCA to size heating and cooling equipment.

Mass effect: Describes the effect of high-mass materials on heating or cooling requirements. High-mass materials such as concrete used in floors and/or walls can absorb and store a significant amount of heat that is later released. In some climates (with considerable sunshine, low humidity, and large daily temperature fluctuations), the use of high-mass materials can reduce cooling and heating requirements by delaying the time at which the heat is released into the house.

Mastic: Strong, flexible material that is used to seal ductwork. It has a thick, creamy consistency when applied and is typically the only effective method of sealing ductwork over the long term.

Minimum efficiency requirements for heating, cooling, and water heating: Air conditioners (split systems): 10 SEER; Heat pumps, heating mode: 6.8 HSPF; Gas fired furnace: 78 percent AFUE; Electric water heater: 0.86 EF (50 gallon); Gas-fired water heater: 0.54 EF (40 gallon).

Model Energy Code (MEC): A model code that requires houses to meet certain energy efficiency-related minimums such as insulation levels or energy consumption. Like most building codes, it is adopted on either a state or local basis, if at all, and may be amended.

Optimum value engineering (OVE): See *advanced framing*.

Outgas: The emission of gases from a solid material as it ages, decomposes, or cures.

Passive solar design: A method of building design that uses the sun's energy for heating and cooling (shading). Features that take advantage of the climate are typically integrated into the building structure and not operated by mechanical means.

Perm rating: A measure of the ability of a material to permit or retard the diffusion of water vapor. A perm, short for permeance, is the number of grains of water vapor that pass through a square foot of material per hour at a differential vapor pressure equal to one inch of mercury.

Photovoltaic (PV): A system that converts sunlight directly to electricity.

Radiant barrier: Typically a foil-faced or foil-like material used in roof systems to reflect radiant heat. When installed properly, radiant barriers can reduce cooling requirements in hot sunny climates.

Radiation (heat flow): The flow of energy across open spaces by electro-magnetic waves such as light. Heat passes from one object to another without warming the air space in between.

Raised-heel roof truss : An engineered roof framing system that rests high enough above the ceiling to allow a continuous, thick blanket of insulation across the entire ceiling surface.

R-value: Measure of the resistance of a material to heat flow.

Sealed combustion furnace: Furnaces that draw air for combustion from outside the home directly into the burner compartment and vent exhaust gases directly outside. The systems eliminate the possibility of backdrafting and the need for a dedicated fresh air inlet into the building.

Seasonal energy efficiency ratio (SEER): A measure of the amount of cooling provided by a central air conditioner per unit of electricity purchased, tested over the entire cooling season. The higher the SEER number, the more efficient the air conditioner. SEER, in contrast to EER, takes into account the efficiency losses resulting from system cycling (on-off operation).

Sensible heat: Released or absorbed heat that has an accompanying temperature change.

Sizing: Calculation of the heat loss and heat gain for a building at "design temperatures" (those close to the maximum and minimum temperatures projected for a given location) in order to select heating and cooling equipment of sufficient capacity. Installing excess equipment capacity, or "oversizing," occurs frequently but leads to inefficient operation and, for air conditioners, decreases the dehumidification. Calculations are most often performed according to the ACCA Manual-J (or similar) procedure.

Solar heat gain coefficient (SHGC): The fraction of sunlight that passes through a window; a measure of how well a product admits heat from incident solar radiation. SHGC is expressed as a number between 0 and 1. A lower SHGC means less heat gain from solar energy.

Structural insulated panel (SIP): Load-bearing wall, roof, or floor panel made of foam sandwiched between two sheets of plywood or oriented strand board (OSB).

Thermal envelope: The protective shell of a building that separates the inside environment from the outside environment. The envelope includes both an insulation layer and an air infiltration layer.

Thermal mass: Heavy materials such as masonry that can store heat energy over a long period and prevent large temperature fluctuations within a home.

Unconditioned space: Space in the home, such as a garage or attic, that is uninsulated and not intended to be heated or cooled or used as a living space. Such areas typically include crawl spaces, attics, and garages.

U-factor: Measure of how readily a material transfers heat, or the inverse of R-value. The lower the U-factor, the greater is the resistance to heat flow (lower U-factor = higher R-value).

Vapor barrier: A material that prohibits moisture from passing through it. The ability of a material to inhibit moisture diffusion is expressed by the material's perm rating. The higher the perm rating, the more vapor that can pass through a material.

Ventilation: The flow of air into or out of a building either mechanically or naturally.

Watt: A unit of measure of instantaneous electric power.

Watt-hour: A unit of measure of electric energy equal to one watt delivered for one hour. A kilowatt-hour (kWh) is equal to 1,000 watt-hours.

Xeriscaping: Landscaping designed to conserve water. Usually involves the use of native, drought-tolerant, hardy plants.